Critical Race Theory

Impact on Black Minority Ethnic Students within Higher Education

I0125251

Critical Race Theory

Impact on Black Minority Ethnic Students within Higher Education

Dilshad Sarwar

TRANSNATIONAL PRESS LONDON
2020

Society and Politics Series: 2

Critical Race Theory: Impact on Black Minority Ethnic Students within Higher Education

Dilshad Sarwar

Copyright © 2020 Transnational Press London

First Published in 2020 by TRANSNATIONAL PRESS LONDON in the United Kingdom, 12 Ridgeway Gardens, London, N6 5XR, UK.
www.tplondon.com

Transnational Press London® and the logo and its affiliated brands are registered trademarks.

Requests for permission to reproduce material from this work should be sent to: sales@tplondon.com

Paperback
ISBN: 978-1-912997-46-6

Cover Design: Nihal Yazgan

www.tplondon.com

CONTENT

ABOUT THE AUTHOR

Dr Dilshad Sarwar is working within the area of Business Systems and Operations at the Faculty of Business and Law, the University of Northampton. In her previous and present role, she has taught at both Undergraduate and Postgraduate levels and has actively been involved in PhD supervisions.

Dilshad's obtained her PhD from Leeds Beckett University. She also has a Postgraduate Certificate in Research, MA in Education Management and MSc Information Systems, She is a Senior Fellow of the HEA.

Dr Sarwar's current research is broadly within the area of BAME Policies and Practices, Information Systems and Business Information Systems as a discipline with a focused research interest in the social influences and domains of Internet of Things and Disaster Management Systems, which entails social computing and managing information in the digital age.

1 ACKNOWLEDGEMENT

First and foremost, I would like to thank God for giving me the willpower and ability to complete my PhD successfully. The writing of this book has been one of the most significant challenges I have ever had to face. Without the support, patience and guidance of the following people, the completion of the thesis would not have been possible. I would like to express my heartfelt gratitude to my supervisors and colleagues Dr Muthu Ramachandran, Professor Martin Samy and Dr Jon Tan. I offer my sincere appreciation for their continuous encouragement and support throughout my thesis. I would further like to extend my heartfelt gratitude to Dr Amin Hosseinian-Far, whose support, guidance and insightful comments at the latter end of my work were truly invaluable. Finally and most importantly, I would like to thank my caring, loving and supportive family. Their quiet patience and unwavering love were undeniably the bedrock upon which the past few years of my life have been built. My family's tolerance is a testament in itself of their unyielding devotion and love. I thank my family for their continuous faith in me and for allowing me to be as ambitious as I wanted. Their encouragement when times got tough is much appreciated and duly noted. To all of you who have supported me along my journey through the good and bad times, I sincerely thank you.

List of Abbreviations

ABS Australian Bureau of Statistics

AEP Australian Education Policy

BME Black Minority Ethnic

BERA British Educational Research Association

CRT Critical Race Theory

ECU Equality Challenge Unit

HEA Higher Education Academy

HEI Higher Education Institutions

HEFCE Higher Education Funding Council for England

HESA Higher Education Statistics Agency

LSA Learning and Skills

QAA Quality Assurance Agency for Higher Education

SIF Social Inclusion Framework Model

UCAS Universities and Colleges Admissions Services

WP Widening Participation

PREFACE

Andrew Pilkington[*]

Research over the last two decades demonstrates that individuals from minority ethnic communities continue disproportionately to experience adverse outcomes. While there is some variability by ethnic group since BMEs are by no means a homogeneous category, BME staff and students experience considerable disadvantage (Arday & Mirza, 2018; Pilkington, 2020). BME academic staff are more likely to be on fixed term contracts, continue to experience significant disadvantage in career progression, especially in gaining access to professorships and the senior ranks of university management, and there remains an ethnic pay gap two decades after the publication of the Macpherson report. Indeed, a recent report based on interviews with BME staff is sceptical that much has changed in the last 20 years: the vast majority continue to experience subtle racism and feel outsiders in the White space of the Academy (Bhopal, 2018). Meanwhile BME students continue to be less likely to be enrolled at elite universities and awarded good honours degrees even when prior attainment and socio-economic status have been taken into account, and to experience lower retention rates and progression rates from undergraduate study to both employment and postgraduate study. A recent inquiry by the Equality and Human Rights Commission found that around a quarter of minority ethnic students had experienced racism since the start of their course and yet many did not feel confident in reporting incidents, not least because of a lack of faith in them being dealt with appropriately. And another investigation by the Guardian confirmed the reluctance of universities to recognise the scale of racism and failure to keep appropriate records. In this context, it is not altogether surprising that minority ethnic students express significantly less satisfaction than their White peers with their university experience.

And yet, despite this evidence of the remarkable persistence in racial disadvantage, universities remain extraordinarily complacent. Such complacency partly stems from the dominance in the academy and indeed of much of society of a liberal as opposed to radical perspective

---

[*] Professor Andrew Pilkington, University of Northampton, UK.

5

on equality. Universities typically see themselves as liberal and believe existing policies ensure fairness; they thus ignore adverse outcomes and do not see combating racial inequalities as a priority. The Chief Executive of the Office for Students (the body which since 2018-19 now distributes government higher education funding for teaching and has taken over from OFFA responsibility for fair access) even acknowledges such 'complacency' in the sector (Batty quoted in Pilkington, 2020). Such inertia will remain intact unless significant pressure is placed on universities to change. Since the early noughties, the salience of race equality as a policy priority has steadily waned with the result that remarkably few initiatives have been mounted within the Academy to promote race equality.

This book arrives at a timely moment. The resurgence of the Black Lives Matter movement in the wake of widespread shock felt across the world over the murder of George Floyd at the hands of the police in the US has triggered a renewed concern with race equality and encouraged organisations, including universities, to reflect on what they are doing to address this issue. While we shall have to wait to see whether fine words are translated into effective actions, there is little doubt that universities are currently more willing to listen to BME voices.

Since 1998, governments of different persuasions have continued to claim widening participation to be a priority and typically have seen policy in this field as the chief means for addressing race equality in higher education. This book examines the impact of this national policy in three very different institutions (an FE college, a pre-1992 university and a post-1992 university) on BME students. The author reminds us that, in the formulation of national policy, the primary focus is on social disadvantage in general rather than racial disadvantage specifically. It is perhaps not altogether surprising in this context that the implementation of this policy at institutional level (which itself differs by institution and is primarily focused on outreach work) does not meet the needs of BME students. The author goes further, however. After analyzing key documents, interviewing staff responsible for WP and conducting focus groups with BME students in her three case study institutions, Dilshad uncovers disturbing evidence of racism and in the process demonstrates how premature it is to claim that the institutional racism identified in the MacPherson report in 1999 and acknowledged by the government at the time has been eradicated. This is a truly shocking indictment. After over 20 years of the implantation of a policy which purportedly promotes race equality, many BME students feel unsupported, isolated and marginal. The author draws upon the framework of critical race theory not only to detail the continuing disadvantages faced by BME students but also utilises this framework to develop a socially inclusive model for action. We need to listen. It is high time that universities were shaken out of their complacency. This book helps us to do just that.

References

Arday, J & Mirza, H (2018). *Dismantling Race in Higher Education*, Basingstoke: Palgrave.

Bhopal, K. (2018). *White Privilege*. Bristol: Policy Press.

Pilkington, A (2020). 'Promoting race equality and supporting ethnic diversity in the Academy: The UK experience over two decades'. In: G. Crimmins (ed.) *Strategies for Supporting Inclusion and Diversity in the Academy*, Basingstoke: Palgrave.

CHAPTER 1

INTRODUCTION

This chapter focuses on identifying CRT within government policy documentation. There is an attempt here by the author to analyse documentation at macro, meso and micro levels. The author furthermore looks to identify methods used at institutional level in terms of how BME issues are addressed through Widening Participation and HEI policies (Caspers, 2019). The twist here is that the author attempts to look at these areas through the lens of CRT and thus the author has developed a framework model for HEIs and Government Bodies to implement (Allen, 2017). The model developed by the author is known as the Social Inclusion Framework Model (SIF) and is demonstrated in figure one below:

Figure 1. A diagrammatical representation of themes

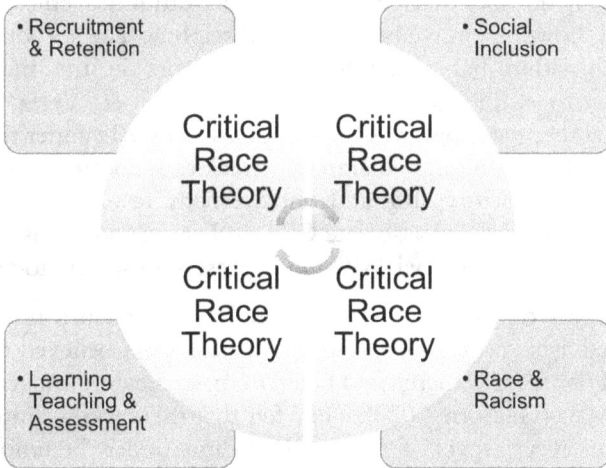

Authors own elaboration – through concept mapping

There is a belief that widening participation is driven and initiated fundamentally at the government level (Blaisdell, 2019). The author has analysed and applied government policy documentation and institutional policy documentation to establish the notion of

1   consistency between both areas (Graham, et al., 2019). It is important
2   to point out here that government policies are thrust upon HEIs and
3   there is limited if any consultation with the key stakeholders, for
4   example, students and academics (Barnes, 2016). Through the research
5   work carried out by the author, it was established that policy
6   documentation is essentially used as a tool to camouflage the meagre
7   practice exercised within HEIs (Anyon, Lechuga, Downing, Greer, &
8   Simmons, 2018).

9   Historically, CRT follows the notion that there is considerable
10   White bias evident in education and society generally (Bimper, 2017).
11   Studies carried out by Ladson Billings believe that there is clear
12   marginalisation regarding students coming from a BME background
13   and in particular, those students for whom English is not their first
14   language (Carrera, 2019). The author further examined the start of the
15   movement for CRT. CRT began when a small group of activists wanted
16   to understand better race, racism and power (Allen, 2017). The first real
17   CRT movement began by focusing their attention on issues relating to
18   conventional civil rights and ethnic study discourses which existed.
19   They began by really questioning the liberal order addressing equality
20   theory, legal reasoning, rationalism and the fundamental principles of
21   constitutional law in America (Dixon, James, & Frieson, 2018).
22   Regardless of the fact that CRT originated from a movement within
23   Law, it did, however, move beyond that discipline. The author further
24   established within her research that educators in the main link
25   themselves to CRT quite holistically (Garcia & Velez, 2018).
26   Educational theorists apply CRT quite loosely to HEIs under the guise
27   of school discipline and hierarchy, tracking, controversies over
28   curriculum and history, IQ and achievement testing. Educational
29   theorists do consider and associate CRT and endeavour to use its core
30   principles to change the social situations present in society today.

31   The origins of CRT began in the mid-1970s when a number of
32   lawyers, activists and legal scholars across the USA believed that the
33   1960s civil rights movements had failed to make any real impact on the
34   lives of BMEs (Gillborn, 2020). They felt that there was a subtle form
35   of racism in every aspect of society. This came under the umbrella of
36   subtle micro aggressions (Carrera, 2019). The author believed the case
37   of Brown vs Brown was a key deciding that education deteriorates over
38   time for people who are from BME backgrounds (Dixon, James, &
39   Frieson, 2018). CRT historically looks at racism as being the norm and
40   that racism is difficult to prevent and that there can never be a colour-
41   blind world regardless of any policies or practices implemented by

governments, institutions or individuals (Garcia & Velez, 2018). Various government bodies over history have tried to implement initiatives to address CRT constructs within HEIs (Blaisdell, 2019). Regardless of a number of initiatives by the main political parties namely Labour and Conservative governments, there has been a fundamental mismatch in aligning widening participation initiatives with CRT and thus failing to create a more constructive format for HEIs to adhere to in relation to BME student cohorts. A further point to note here is that HEIs have continued to operate with an elitist nature. Over history, the elitist nature of HEIs has been evident in both redbrick Universities and that of post 92 Universities.

Government Strategy

The government strategy from both the Conservative and Labour governments was always implemented on the basis of wanting to create an effective learning environment within HEIs for non-traditional students. The views held by government bodies have, in essence, attempted to create drive and initiatives which HEIs have not been held accountable for, meaning that in many respects HEIs have to a large extent been able to interpret widening participation and BME student recruitment and retention (Hawkins, Carter-Francique, & Cooper, 2016). Again historically, four key areas were considered essential within HEIs in respect to raising standards of educational attainment, secondly raise aspirations of BME students, thirdly improve the admissions processes within the view of increasing the number of BME students within HEIs (Allen, 2017).

Government Initiatives for Widening Participation

According to government strategy, the main influx was to ensure that HEIs were moving towards widening participation and in a more positive format (Hurtardo, 2019). Supporting initiatives involving BME students (Goessling, 2018). The author during the study outlined that Widening participation within Universities was an avenue to accommodate the social mix of students, if and only if HEIs were happy to fully embrace BME non-traditional students into the sphere of higher education. This study showed significantly that achieving equality within HEIs was deemed difficult regardless of any government policy and process being implemented. The concepts such as 'Equal Opportunity', 'Access' and 'Equity' are central to the analysis of any form of BME participation within HEIs. There is considerable importance here that signifies the findings of the study (Adams, 2017). As HEIs were once designed for an elite group of students, its agenda

1   provides considerable challenges to establishing clear diversity and
2   equality (Hawkins, Carter-Francique, & Cooper, 2016). Even in the
3   21st Century, there is a considerable amount of work that is still
4   required to be established in view of the governmental policies and
5   practices in place. A number of government Race Relations and
6   Disability legislation initiatives have been included but not been
7   completely successful within HEI inclusion of BME students
8   (Moodley, Mujtaba, & Kleiman, 2017). The amended Race Relations
9   Act and the Special Educational Needs and Discrimination Act (2001),
10   focus on approaches which institutions need to take to redress the
11   systematic institutional exclusion faced by disabled people and people
12   from BME communities (Jackson & Barton, 2017).

CHAPTER 2

CRITICAL RACE THEORY AN EDUCATIONAL CONSTRUCT

Historical Perspectives of Critical Race Theory

Critical Race Theory (CRT) was founded in America and extraordinarily from the Law Society. Legal studies during the post-civil rights movement and developed from a real sense of frustration CRT was born (Flores, 2017). Moreover, a number of themes which were associated with CRT in law focused on a significant attack on the United States Supreme Courts view in relation to race and racial equality, in particular when dealing with black concerns (Lee, Harrell, Villarreal, & White, 2020). The author furthermore, highlights the view that CRT goes beyond the Black and White paradigms (Johnson-Ahorlu, 2017). The origins of CRT can thus date back to the 1980s where the political, intellectual and sociological developments in the American legislative system. Politically 1980s witnessed the American Civil Rights Activists and the left-wing legal scholars in a conservative backlash against the gains of the 1960s.

As a result, scholars became known as CRT theorists who were finding reasoning behind why there was only limited success in improving the experiences of African Americans and other Non-Whites, and why social integration with White people was seen as limited within society (Perez Huber & Solorzano, 2018). The gradual entrance of African Americans in academia and other Non-Whites did little to stamp out the CRT theorists viewpoints.

Ladson Billings' in work written in 1995 outlined the clear concepts of Critical Race Theory (CRT), highlighting the impact of CRT within everyday life and within society including the Education sector (Perez Huber & Solorzano, 2018). CRT was implemented to address the imbalance and injustice witnessed by many non-white individuals. CRT was first developed to address and reduce and attempt to prevent existing racism patterns evident in society. Thus CRT theorists believed that racism is in fact, difficult to define or eradicate (Bimper, 2017). CRT encompasses the notion that racism surpasses white elites, the working classes, making it therefore very difficult to eradicate racism.

13

1 CRT further compounds the view that the focus is laid bare in terms
2 of the political struggles which are necessary for racial justice. In
3 essence, there is a pragmatist and utopian vision which draws on critical
4 strategies that illustrate how the legal viewpoints create a disadvantage
5 for those individuals of colour (Rosiek, 2019). CRT theorists believe
6 that racism is ordinary and a normal part of contemporary society and
7 that CRT is embedded within the norms of society and in particular
8 prevalent within HEIs (Singer & Garner, 2017). The notion of CRT
9 within HEIs is one of collective denial. Furthermore, the US state not
10 addressing the perpetration of racism within its society advocates the
11 fact that does the US state accepts the term racism and that racism is
12 seen as the norm and does not require addressing (Sablan, 2019). CRT
13 theorists believe that there is an endeavour to show how contemporary
14 law which includes the view that racism is accommodated within
15 society (Parker, 2019). CRT activists are coherent in the notion that
16 although racism should be challenged, it is in fact, a permanent feature
17 within society. CRT theorists furthermore are under the notion that the
18 theory of implicit bias is required in order to successfully reshape anti
19 discriminatory law. Scholars have long argued that CRT is aimed at
20 pursuing the view that innovations such as the theory of implicit bias
21 can be used successfully to reshape anti-discriminatory law into a more
22 effective tool against racism (Adams, 2017).

23 CRT has identified the continuity of racial oppression across a
24 number of years despite the changes in the legal and political arenas.
25 Through a number of CRT studies, it was quite clear that the most
26 recognised CRT study was that of Brown vs Board of Education the
27 most notorious court case in which the court declared that state laws
28 building and establishing separate public schools for Black and White
29 students were deemed unconstitutional (Mattews, 2019). This court
30 case evidently has clear significance within the American Schools.
31 From this, a charter has been developed with a clear narrative implicit
32 on preservation through transformation (Saito & Kinnison, 2020).

33 CRT theorists even today, however, are still of the belief that racism
34 is constantly changing in form but not effect within society (Kennedy,
35 2017). Further studies by CRT theorists also conform to the view that
36 the government bodies can legitimately use Race as a form of enforcing
37 immigration laws (Lavender, 2019). CRT theorists are in agreement
38 that there is an intention to discriminate against BME individuals
39 regardless of a White individuals desire to be or not to be racist. CRT
40 theorists argue that unconsciously White individuals are racist.

1   CRT theorists furthermore believe that racism is multidimensional.
2   A clear example here is where Latinos within America and Aborigines
3   living in Australia have been under considerable disadvantage under
4   the educational system, where inter-sectionalisim is commonplace
5   (Saito & Kinnison, 2020). Research studies undertaken by Ladson-
6   Billings in 1995 suggested that CRT is very evident within HEIs. Other
7   works written by Ladson-Billings in 1990 discusses how knowledge is
8   defined, which individuals knowledge sharing is counted and which
9   individuals is discounted. To further support CRT theorists, works
10   completed by Bourdieu and Passeron in 1977 outline that CRT
11   articulates the view that social inequality, is based on the paradigm of a
12   racist society. The belief that BME individuals are restricted by the
13   social and cultural capital required for social mobility are further
14   emphasised through research undertaken by Bourdieu.

15   An additional consequence of this is within educational
16   establishments in the assumption that BME students lack the necessary
17   knowledge, social skills, abilities and cultural capital to succeed. The
18   theoretical perspectives of CRT are very pertinent when considering
19   BME individuals within HEIs (Howard & Navarro, 2016). CRT
20   theorists further articulate that academic and social outcomes for BME
21   students are significantly lower. This notion was further supported by
22   Ladson-Billings academic underpinning in 2000. BME students are
23   always considered as lacking necessary knowledge, social skills, abilities
24   and cultural capital.

25   **Figure 2**. Intellectual Genealogy of Critical Race Theory

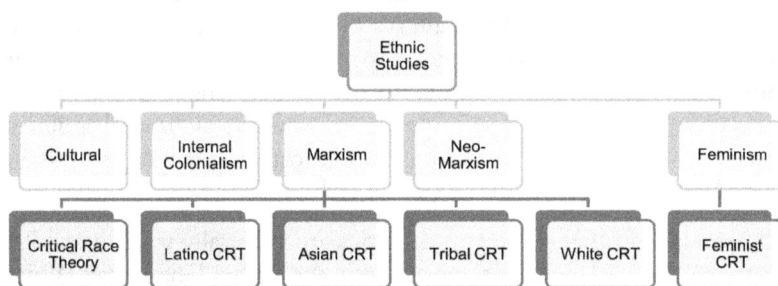

26

27   CRT theorists clearly believe that racism towards BMEs is not
28   simply justified in terms of Black and White cultural differences
29   (Richards, Awokoya, Bridges, & Clark, 2018). Within the realms of
30   BME students, CRT adds to measures which continue to recognise the

1   ways in which there is still a struggle for social justice and the limited
2   discourses that omit or silence BME students. Race and Racism is very
3   much embedded within CRT in terms of how society functions (Yao,
4   George, & Malaney, 2019). One of the fundamental arguments is that
5   CRT challenges White privilege and opposes the claims that HEIs
6   make towards objectivity, meritocracy, colour blindness, race neutrality
7   and equal opportunities (Annamma, Ferri, & Connor, 2018). CRT
8   argues that traditional claims are a disguise for the self-interest of the
9   White middle classes. The author believes that CRT within HEIs
10 challenges the ways race and racism impact educational structures,
11 practices, discourses, underpinned through ongoing research studies
12 carried out by Ladson-Billing (Ladson-Billings, 2009). CRT challenges
13 White privilege and opposes the claims that HEIs make towards
14 objectivity, meritocracy, colour blindness, race neutrality and equal
15 opportunity as this was evident in research undertaken by Ladson-
16 Billings. CRT theorists believe that traditional claims are a disguise for
17 the self-interest of the White middle classes. CRT is very much
18 committed to social justice and draws on the lived experiences and
19 understanding of BME individuals. CRT within education challenges
20 the ways race and racism impact educational structures, practices and
21 discourses, underpinned by studies carried out by CRT theorists such
22 as Ladson-Billing.

23   Cultural influences on how society is organised and how HEI
24 curriculum is embedded with racism and the lack of pedagogy and
25 policy representing BME students are significant in the undermining of
26 BME students (Singer & Garner, 2017). Studies by Bourdieu discuss
27 the concepts which state BME students attainment is embedded with
28 the notion that BME students always perform poorly in their overall
29 teaching, learning and assessment experience in comparison to their
30 White middle class peers. Bourdieu further argues that cultural capital
31 refers to an accumulation of cultural knowledge, skills and abilities
32 possessed and inherited by White, middle class privileged groups in
33 society (Stovell, 2016).

34   The assertion that some communities are culturally wealthy, whilst
35 others are deemed culturally poor, with the norm being that White
36 middle-class culture and all other cultures are deemed as poor in terms
37 of knowledge and understanding particularly in terms of HEI learning
38 (Walls, 2016). Moreover, BMEs are deemed as having poor cultural
39 capital, whereas White middle-class students are considered as rich in
40 cultural capital which is beneficial for them within HEI environments.
41 For this reason, CRT theorists believe that there is a need to shift the

1   balance and to improve BME overall HEI experiences.

2   **Figure 3.** A Community of Wealth through CRT ideology

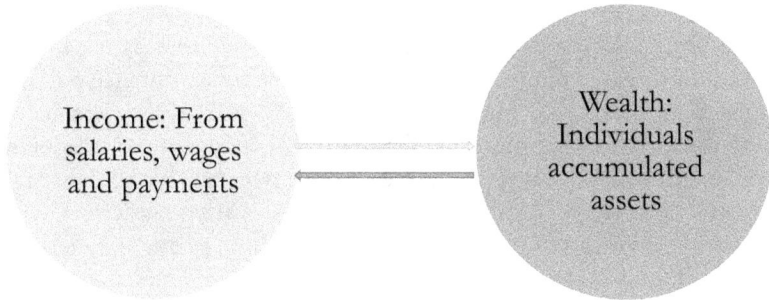

3

4   **Figure 4.** A model of community cultural wealth

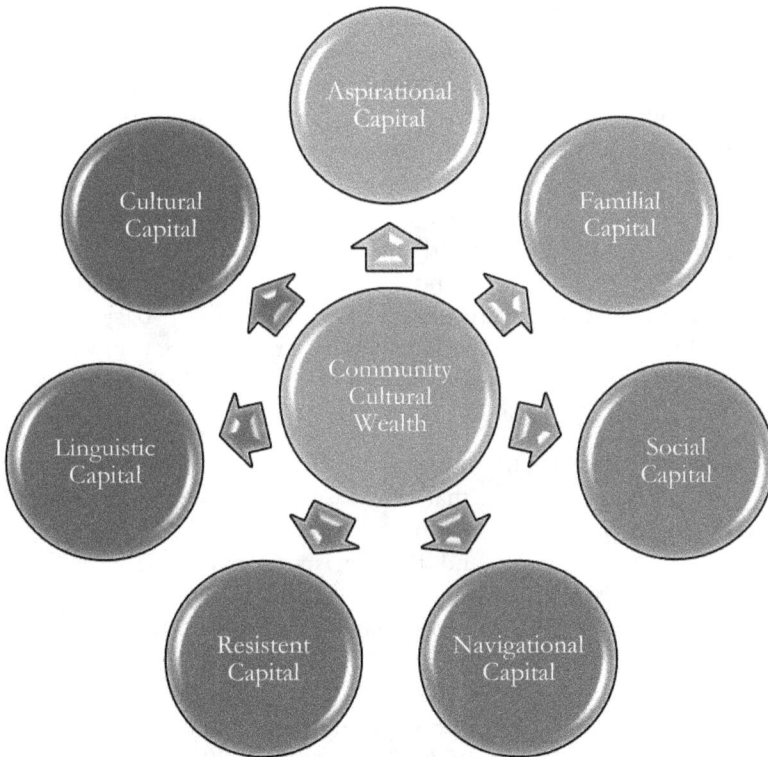

5

1   Figures 3 and 4 outline areas that are considered to be essential for
2   intellectual and social inclusion for BMEs. Moreover, HEIs social
3   inclusion measures in terms of BME students start their studies with
4   English as their second language (Walls, 2016). The author believes that
5   HEI unknowingly or perhaps knowingly are isolating BME students as
6   they do not easily fit into the HEI community and culture. Navigational
7   capital is outlined in figure 4 which stipulates the disadvantaged cultural
8   environments HEIs are for BME students (Allen, 2017). Strategies to
9   move through HEI campuses draw on the concept of academic
10   vulnerabilities and BME students lack of ability to be able to gain high
11   levels of academic achievement in their learning, teaching and
12   assessment environments (Trazo & Kim, 2019). It seems through the
13   detailed analysis carried out by the author BME students are seen as
14   having considerable knowledge however, regardless of this their
15   experiences, cultural and languages are devalued when they enter HEIs
16   (Yao, George, & Malaney, 2019). Within the politics of education there
17   is an assumption that individuals regardless of colour have certain
18   inalienable rights. The author believes that within the politics of
19   education, there is an assumption that individuals act in politically
20   rational ways and will assert their rights as citizens through influence,
21   power, conflict, political pressure, voting, or some other mechanism
22   (Reynolds & Mayweather, 2017). Unfortunately, the vast majority of
23   people of colour, the working poor, women and marginalised groups
24   who are constantly reminded of their second-class status (Mensah,
25   2019). It has also been identified that almost over twenty years ago
26   racism was active in the UK and has actually never waned despite
27   government mandates that prohibit discrimination on the basis of race
28   (Daftary, 2018). The only difference between racism today and of the
29   past is that modern day racism is more subtle, invisible and insidious.

30   Popular beliefs such as colour blindness and equal opportunity have
31   only served to drive racism underground (Perez Huber & Solorzano,
32   2018). CRT theorists believe that the reason why society fails to see
33   racism is because it is such a common and everyday experience that it
34   is often taken for granted and that racism is part of society and
35   embedded in HEI organisations, practices, and structures (Lavender,
36   2019). The authors study further applied the view that racism shapes
37   the HEIs relationships and the way White middle classes think and
38   behave towards BMEs (Rector-Aranda). CRT actually unmasks the
39   hidden views of racism, a notion supported and analysed extensively
40   through the authors research study (Trazo & Kim, 2019).

41   When observed holistically, the CRT theorists put into perspective

1   that the notion of neutrality, democracy, objectivity and equality are not
2   only unattainable ideals, which are harmful fictions that obscure the
3   normative supremacy of Whiteness within HEIs (James & Russell,
4   2019). The belief that politics of education actively supports a racist
5   agenda does not fit the constructs that HEIs should hold. The role of
6   CRT is to really highlight the fact that such beliefs only serve to
7   maintain racism in place, but moving racism to overt and clear acts of
8   hatred, as opposed to highlighting the ways in which BME beliefs,
9   practices, knowledge and apparatuses reproduce a system of racial
10   hierarchy and social inequality (Walls, 2016). BME students are
11   continuously seen as failures regardless of their abilities and
12   competence (Singer & Garner, 2017). Thus, the notion of mainstream
13   society has not altered the viewpoint of wishing to see BME students
14   fail and this concept is engrained within HEIs.

15   Further analysis by CRT theorists outlines the fact that there is a
16   requirement to develop a framework model in order to address
17   educational inequality within HEIs (Gillborn, 2020). Race it is believed
18   plays a fundamental factor of inequality within HEIs where it is clearly
19   witnessed that race is seen as a fundamental factor of inequality
20   (Gilborn, Warmington, & Denmack, 2018). Rather than finding and
21   providing an improved educational structure for BME students there
22   seems to be greater alienation and reduced levels of social inclusion
23   (Giraldo, Huerta, & Solorzano, 2017).

24

CHAPTER 3

RESEARCH METHODOLOGY

This study is the first academically documented attempt to research BME students' participation at national, institutional and operational level policy documentation in terms of the impact on three case study HEIs, which is significantly aimed at social inclusion for BME students in the UK educational system, resulting in the development of the Social Inclusion Framework model (SIF) (Barnes, 2016). The purpose of this study has been to create a more focused widening participation framework model (SIF). Contextual experiences are developed from the research approach used by the researcher and this is based on the values and contextual experiences gained by the researcher (Anderson & Shattuck, 2013). Social science research works across diverse disciplines and therefore not defined by one theoretical concept. This Chapter establishes the framework and methods adopted to complete the research study (Henson, Hull, & Williams, 2010). Fundamental qualitative research methods and framework analysis are formulated within the research design. Research questions are examined further when establishing the approaches adopted for this study. The literature is then related to previous Chapters which will support the development of the framework model (SIF). The conceptual framework is examined, critiquing the research product and the research process (Henson, Hull, & Williams, 2010). Finally, an extensive exploration of ethics in research is discussed detailing how the study was progressed within the ethical framework. Social, political and economic factors are imperative areas of analysis whereby critical race theory is embedded within the contextualisation of fundamental themes within this study of recruitment and retention, social inclusion, learning teaching and assessment and race and racism.

1 **Figure 5.** Diagrammatical Representation of Fundamental Themes in
2 the Study

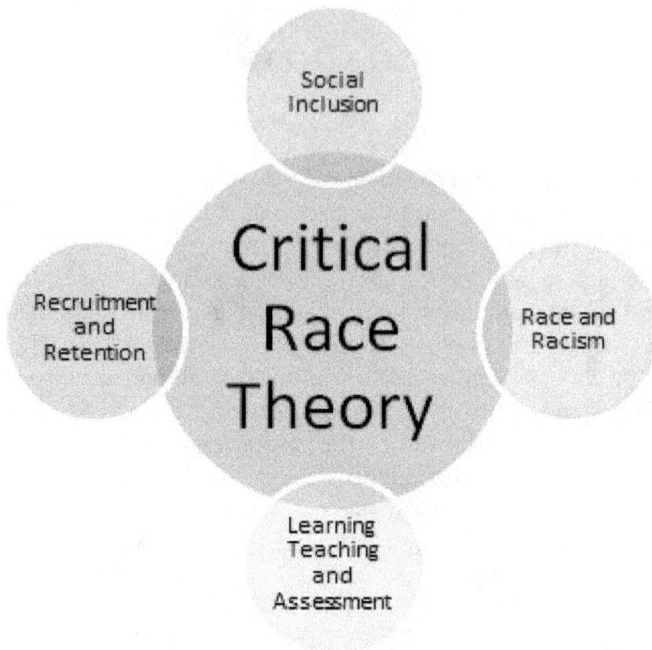

3

4   The purpose of this study has been to create a more focused
5 widening participation framework model Social Inclusion Framework
6 Model (SIF) which will address the following research questions
7 outlined in Chapter one, the questions stated below are central to the
8 study:

9   •   National Policy Documents

10   How do national level government policies inform the
11   widening participation practices for BME minority ethnic
12   students in higher education? (document analysis)

13   •   Institutional Level Policy Documents

14   How do Higher Education (HEIs) translate and apply the
15   national widening participation policies for BME minority
16   ethnic students and put their policies into practice in terms
17   of social Inclusion – What methods are used by HEIs to
18   ensure social inclusion occurs within the institution?
19   (document analysis, interviews)

- Operational Level Policy Documents

  Are the administrative staff and academic staff at the case study HEIs translating the institutional level widening participation policies into practice for BME minority ethnic students?

  Does the widening participating policy fit into the student admissions policy within the context of social inclusion what measures are taken at Course, Module, Teaching, Learning and Assessment level to ensure social inclusion is being addressed?

  Are structures in place for the recruitment and retention of BME students and do the case study HEIs have clear policies in place at admissions level to address the recruitment of BME student's?

  Do BME minority ethnic students believe that they are supported during their time at university?

  At HEI level, have widening participation policies supported BME minority ethnic students teaching, learning and assessments throughout university? (Interviews and document analysis)

Research design

The study concentrates on widening participation framing surrounding BME students. The study addresses HEI widening participation commitment in association with the social inclusion of BME students. Three case study HEIs have been selected as post-92 (HEI A), Further Education College (HEI B) and pre-92 (HEI C).

The HEIs were selected on the basis of the following points:

- Organisational structure

- Admissions

- Historical context

- Regional context

Russell Group HEIs have a selective admissions procedure which is not positioned towards widening participation (Younger, Gascoine, Menzies, & Torgerson, 2019). The three selected case study HEI staff and students agreed to participate in this study, and form the basis of

1   findings and conclusions outlined in Chapter seven. In-depth semi-
2   structured interviews were carried out with staff and students. Ten staff
3   members were selected from the case study HEIs and thirty students
4   were selected from each of the case study HEIs. The conceptual
5   framework developed in this study provides a detailed analysis into the
6   difficult and somewhat complex understanding of widening
7   participation in the context of BME students (Moodley, Mujtaba, &
8   Kleiman, 2017). The conceptual framework model developed within
9   this study will be put forward as the model to be implemented by the
10   three case study HEIs.

11   **Qualitative Research**

12   Before a decision was formalised in relation to the research
13 approach followed, both qualitative and quantitative research
14 approaches were investigated. Qualitative research approach
15 techniques are applied for this study. Figure 6 below looks at the
16 Qualitative approaches:

17   **Figure 6.** Qualitative Research Overview Adapted

Qualitative Research

- **Assumptions**
  - Reality is socially constructed
  - Variables are complex and interwoven
  - Events are viewed from informants' perspectives
  - Dynamic reality to life
- **Purpose**
  - Interpretation
  - Contextualisation
  - Understanding the perspectives of others
  - Theory building
- **Method**
  - Data collection using interviews
  - Concludes with hypothesis
  - Emergence and portrayal
  - Thematic analysis
  - findings idiographic
  - Data and rich data
  - Focus on authenticity
- **Researcher:** used as an instrument
  - personal involvement
  - Empathic understanding

18   Source: Miles & Huberman (1994)

19   Assumptions are relevant to the methodological approach taken by
20 the researcher as the view of reality being socially constructed is in

1 essence imperative to the research study. The variables are complex
2 and interwoven as depicted in Figure 6 signify the depth of interviews
3 and analysis which underpinned the research study (Younger,
4 Gascoine, Menzies, & Torgerson, 2019). The questions asked within
5 interviews were based on the interviewees' responses. The staff and
6 students interviewed were able to place a significant degree of reality to
7 the study, as real life experiences were discussed by the interviewees.
8 The purpose of using the qualitative research methodology as depicted
9 in Figure 7 contextualises and enables the interviewer to gain a clear
10 understanding of the perspectives of others, through the interpretation
11 and theory building process. The method used for this study involved
12 data collection using semi-structured interview. As Figure 6 outlines,
13 thematic analysis is significant throughout the study, with the use of
14 ideographics within the findings the researcher was able to look at two
15 different approaches to understanding social life. The researcher has
16 been used as an instrument in order to gain key information from the
17 interviewees. Advantages of the qualitative approach include the
18 researcher being able to gain full insight into the subject matter,
19 allowing social interaction between the interviewer and participants.
20 The positive aspects of qualitative research are that the method allows
21 for intricate detail to be obtained from the participants. Qualitative
22 research approach fits well within studies that are considering social
23 research analysis.

24 Furthermore, the qualitative research method does allow for a
25 closer relationship to develop between the researcher and the
26 participants and is an excellent means of examining societal
27 ideographics. The qualitative methodology is a fundamental method
28 within social science research. The researcher has, at length, analysed
29 extensively the epistemological stance in relation to qualitative research.
30 The researcher examined qualitative methods when deciding on a
31 chosen methodological approach to adapt. The researcher established
32 that for this research, the qualitative approach would be more specific.
33 In-depth analysis is a move towards the qualitative approach as human
34 relations based on the levels of trust cannot be measured therefore the
35 quantitative approach was not deemed suitable. The quantitative
36 approach does not best fit within social science realm. The qualitative
37 research approach is more suitable for studies involving human
38 participants.

Qualitative research approach

40 Social science attempts to address a multitude of perspectives,

1   which provide a variety of methods to gather and analyse data.
2   Qualitative research refers to social inquiry which at its best investigates
3   social constructs. Qualitative research is separated from other methods
4   by inductive and deductive approaches. Deductive approaches
5   establish meaning from examination from data set, whereas inductive
6   approaches stem from building meaning from examining the
7   information available within the context of the research. Under
8   qualitative research, various research methods are incorporated. For
9   this study case study and interview will be discussed in order to clarify
10   how these two approaches are relevant to the study (Anderson &
11   Shattuck, 2013).

12   Both deductive and inductive approaches were used in this study.
13   Deductive reasoning operates from the perspective of the general to
14   the specific areas of research. This approach is considered as a "top
15   down" methodology. In terms of deductive reasoning the theoretical
16   concepts outlined in the research are then streamlined into a more,
17   focused hypothesis that the researcher can then assess (Garcia & Velez,
18   2018). Once the process has been outlined, it moves to the analysis of
19   specific data which confirms or dismisses the original theory which was
20   outlined. Inductive reasoning functions differently in the sense that
21   specific observations can be related to broader generalised theories.
22   This "bottom up" approach in inductive reasoning will detect
23   consistencies and regularities, this allows the researcher to formulate
24   some immediate hypotheses that the researcher can examine further
25   the hypotheses and from that exploration be able to develop general
26   conclusions and theories (Case & Light, Emerging research
27   methodologies in engineering education reseearch. , 2011).

28   Both deductive and inductive reasoning methods were used by the
29   researcher as this study focuses on policies from a macro, meso and
30   then micro level and additionally looks at the bottom up approach of
31   micro, meso and macro levels.

32   Inductive reasoning allowed the researcher to be more focussed on
33   open-ended and exploration which is very evident at the start of the
34   research (Kennedy, 2017). The researcher used deductive reasoning in
35   order to establish a more streamlined process which allowed for the
36   testing and confirming of the hypotheses.

37   Qualitative research is multi-method in focus, involving an
38   interpretive, naturalistic approach to its subject matter. This means that
39   qualitative researchers study things in their natural settings, attempting
40   to make sense of or interpret phenomena in terms of the meanings

people bring to them. Qualitative research involves the studied use and collection of a variety of empirical materials case study, personal experience, introspective, life story interview, observational, historical, interactional, and visual texts-that describe routine and problematic moments and meaning in individuals' lives (Henson, Hull, & Williams, 2010). Qualitative research is an inquiry process of understanding based on distinct methodological traditions of inquiry that explore a social or human problem. The researcher builds a complex, holistic picture, analyses words, reports detailed views of informants and conducts the study in a natural setting (Sablan, 2019). Qualitative or interpretive research enables the researcher to consider approaches in which particular situations and gain understanding to social meaning (Spinuzzi, 2005). Qualitative researchers do recognise the risk to reliability; however, the use of triangulation can respond to this concern. Triangulation uses more than one approach to establish confidence in the findings. The concept of triangulation is associated with the measurement practice within the realms of social research. Data triangulation allows for:

- Data triangulation which allows for the bringing together of data through a degree of sampling strategies state that data can be different at various times. Additional analysis can be included in accordance with the individuals involved within the research. For this study it was imperative for validity and authenticity that data obtained from interviews were triangulated.

- Investigatory triangulation associates itself with more than one researcher. As the researcher through an extensive literature review analysed other research studies, this was significant when carrying out interviews for authenticity.

- Theoretical triangulation focuses on theoretical positioning when interpreting data. Adding theory to the data analysed allowed for the researcher to gain significant insight into methods used to establish validity and reliability.

Triangulation fundamentally allows for the cross examination of data and is considered a strong method that allows and supports validation of data by means of cross verification from a number of sources (Stovall, 2018). Triangulation improves data credibility and validity of findings. Triangulation is considered as an attempt to map out or explain more than one viewpoint. Triangulation allows for a more detailed and structured focus on the situation which is under investigation. Triangulation further removes bias from the data collected. Qualitative research is subjective with the view that different people can perceive the truth differently. The qualitative approach examines aspects such as language and images rather than numerical formats (Moustakas, 1990). This research approach views human perceptions and the way in which the subjects act and interact and in accordance with the complex nature of human beings. This research approach allows the study in which people interpret and represent particular situations and are then able to analyse how social meanings are examined (Turner, Balmer, & Coverdale, 2013). The research study analyses contradictions in national and local policy interpretation that have a considerable impact on social inclusion within the three selected HEIs. Qualitative research takes the form of interviews, focus groups and observations as the methods most suitable to address social situations. The research paradigm incorporated within this study focuses on exploratory research (Turner, Balmer, & Coverdale, 2013). Exploratory research is particularly suitable for this study as the research concentrates on a concept of people and situations. Validity is an important concern associated with any research. There is a fundamental association between integrity and validity.

Qualitative research allows a considerable degree of validity as it is based within the natural setting. As this study involves document analysis of national widening participation policies and the manner in which these policies are then translated at institutional level, framing of widening participation needs to be examined within a natural setting (Zhu, Peng, & Qui, 2019). The natural settings outlined here involve semi-structured interviews with thirty members of staff, ten from each of the three HEIs and ninety focus group interviews (thirty students) from each of the HEIs.

Questions for the research study were developed from generic exploratory interest in social inclusion within higher education. Fundamental significance to this study is to assess the extent of the critical race theory construct within the selected HEIs coupled with social justice model. It is anticipated that the research study will enable the case study HEIs to develop a distinct framework model encompassing social inclusion.

Validity and reliability

Validity is considered as a correct relation to the investigation under study. The research is considered as reliable if the questions asked are repeated and the same phenomena are used throughout the study.

1   Triangulation allows for validity to be achieved. It is imperative that the
2   four varying forms of triangulation are followed. Validation and the
3   enhancement of the focus groups and the exploratory interviews
4   conducted for the research have allowed the researcher gain greater
5   consistency within the findings. The findings from the focus groups
6   have been validated through the use of exploratory interviews as
7   recommended within the literature review. The exploratory interviews
8   conducted focused on fundamental problem areas which have been
9   raised in chapter one. The interviews were used as a means of
10   confirming theory building throughout the study. For this study, the
11   researcher felt it necessary to neglect pre-existing knowledge.

12 ## HEIs case study – comparative methodology

13   Three case study HEIs were approached for this study. Three case
14   study HEIs have been selected as: post-92 (HEI A), Further Education
15   College (HEI B), and pre-92 (HEI C). The study concentrates on
16   widening participation framing surrounding BME students. The study
17   addresses HEI widening participation commitment in association with
18   the social inclusion of BME students. Three case study HEIs have been
19   selected as post 92 (HEI A), Further Education College (HEI B) and
20   pre-92 (HEI C). The HEIs were selected on the basis of the following
21   points:

22   • Organisational structure: all three case study HEIs were
23   considered in terms of the universities' and college
24   departments.

25   • Admissions: the admissions departments for all three case study
26   HEIs were analysed in terms of the provision for BMEs.

27   • Historical context: An analysis of historical context was
28   considered by the researcher before and during the research
29   study.

30   • Regional context: Regional context was paramount to the study
31   as all three case study HEIs are situated within the Yorkshire
32   region. Pseudonyms for all three case study HEIs were used by
33   the researcher.

34   The chosen HEIs have a meaningful contribution to this study. It
35   can be understood that from discursive representations of widening
36   participation there would be a considerable difference in the inclusion
37   of widening participation in the context of social inclusion for BME
38   students (Henson, Hull, & Williams, 2010). With the three selected case

1 study HEIs ten staff were interviewed from each of the HEIs and focus
2 group interviews were carried out with thirty students from each HEI.
3 HEI A is a post 92 HEI and offers both vocational and academic
4 courses to students with a sphere of qualifications.

5 There is a larger intake of non-traditional students within this HEI
6 and the university has a significant track record of commitment to
7 increase widening participation. HEI B is a Further Education College,
8 which has a substantial commitment to widening participation with a
9 large proportion of the student intake coming from under- represented
10 groups in higher education. Many of HEI B students are from the local
11 community, the courses are mainly but not exclusively vocational and
12 research is not considered to be a fundamental feature of the HEI. HEI
13 C belongs to the Russell Group of HEIs with a fundamental focus on
14 research and academic quality, the main student intake consists of A
15 level qualifications, HEI C provides an exclusive plan which is placed
16 amongst world class HEIs. It is important to gain understanding of the
17 HEIs in context to what is occurring within the HEI at the present
18 moment. To accomplish this, interviews were undertaken with the
19 widening participation managers at each HEI. Policy documentation
20 was analysed from all three HEIs to enable a diagnostic understanding
21 of the widening participation policy implemented by the three case
22 study HEIs. Case studies are fundamental to qualitative research, the
23 case study approach is empirically investigated. Open research
24 questions fundamentally lead to data abstractions, where evidence is
25 gathered from a number of different sources in order to allow for the
26 best possible answers to the research questions.

27 **Qualitative research attributes:**

28 • Addresses a particular concern

29 • Real people and situations which are set in real
30 environments

31 • Generalisations appear from the data

32 • New meaning, extending experiences and confirms what is
33 known

34 • Achieves:

35 • Thick descriptive data

36 • Sources participant:

- Observation

- Interviews

- Historical and narrative sources

- Written documents

- Quantitative data

With qualitative data reproducing participants' views with a thorough description of events with accurate reports of actions and settings, the use of triangulation from a number of sources are some of the positive aspects of this method. The negative aspects of this method include the time factor as this method is extremely time consuming. Furthermore the results are not available until the research has been completed. The interpretation of results can be viewed as biased. The case study method has been implemented in this study, the researcher has interpreted the concepts and generalisations in the data, the participants are real people set in their real environments, further the research situation is constructed, the data are from interviews which considered as thick descriptive data.

Three HEIs were selected in examining some of the varied approaches to widening participation and social inclusion with HEIs. This comparative case study approach associates with the use of indistinguishable methods to study contrasting cases. With the use of two or more case studies a substantial theory can be developed. This comparative case study approach involves the study of three HEIs, which have been selected to enable the research questions outlined in chapter one. The case study approach has a number of advantages. This research tool allows for multiple phenomena to be considered at once. The case study approach is particularly relevant to this research and the research questions outlined in chapter one. The allowance for greater understanding gained with the use of the case study approach is far more achievable. This method will further allow the use of triangulation which will increase validity of the findings. With case study research, it is important to understand what is happening at the present time. Widening participation managers and the admissions staff were selected to participate in the study. The widening participation managers were seen as fundamental to the study as they are responsible for ensuring that widening participation policies and practices are being implemented within the HEIs. The information obtained from interviews was then triangulated using data collected through interviews.

Bernstein's framework model

The case study approach allows for a clearer design, data collection technique and detailed approaches to data analysis. The theoretical framework enables the reader to gain a greater understanding of the research questions outlined, and conclusions arrived at. The limitations of the case study approach are defined with the use of theoretical framing. This study is concerned with the institutional framing of social inclusion and widening participation, with the interpretation of national policy documentation and the commitment and interpretation at the institutional and operational level. Perceptions of classification and framing are fundamental to the understanding of how the three case study HEIs have developed their commitment and understanding of widening participation and social inclusion. Bernstein's framework model is based on the concept of how people talk and the methods they use to convey meaning. This framing model outlined by Bernstein is applicable to institutional framing outlined with the analysis of policy documentation, developed through interviews carried out with the staff. Institutional framing contains structured analysis based around creating a clear directive.

Weak framing means poor structure and poor quality within HEIs; fundamentally it means that there are inconsistencies put forward in the widening participation and social inclusion classification. Within any institution, there may be areas of good practice of social inclusion and widening participation coupled with areas within the institution whereby very poor practice is followed. There is weak framing there is inconsistency and incoherence with the message being delivered. With the use of classification, HEIs can stipulate differences with the types of institution the HEIs wish to be considered as. For example, Russell Group HEIs would wish to be seen as different from the post-92 HEIs and place greater emphasis on standards and research.

Post-92 HEIs might wish to be considered as supporting social inclusion and widening participation. With each category, Bernstein believes there are clear and defined identities. To achieve greater control and power, HEIs will want to control what they want to include in policy documentation and what they wish to leave out. HEIs are focusing on creating differentiation between one another and by doing so fundamentally illustrate that classification and framing are linked. Framing, therefore, goes beyond social inclusion and widening participation, however, becomes interdependent on the HEI holistically. National framing (government agenda) of widening

1   participation and social inclusion coupled with local framing (the
2   output of messages from the case study HEIs) are analysed. The
3   fundamental view of the analysis of interview data requires further
4   clarification. Ethno-methodologists do not believe that data pre-exist.
5   Interviews are seen as a method used to make sense of conversations.
6   Further to this constructionists view interviews as a standalone case.
7   Through verbal communication, meaning and information can be
8   obtained.

9   As humans communicate verbally, conversation allows for
10 meaning-making which is experienced by the individuals within the
11 conversation. Knowledge can be communicated through meaningful
12 conversations. Advantages of carrying out interviews in person rather
13 than using questionnaires allow for further exploration of meaning.
14 Three types of interview methods can be conducted, structured, semi-
15 structured and unstructured. Unstructured interviews are driven by the
16 interviewee. The researcher can decipher further information by asking
17 probing questions. Probing can further be included within semi-
18 structured interviews, where there is a list of questions to follow, where
19 the interviewee is provided with the opportunity to raise concerns, ask
20 questions, and provide deeper meaning to the questions. Structured
21 interviews are asked in a specific order, identical questions are asked
22 and a limited amount of responses are documented by a pre-established
23 coding scheme.

24   Individual face-to-face qualitative interviews, focus group
25 interviews are seen as an effective method of observing natural
26 discussion. With focus group interviews, the dynamics of the group can
27 highlight social and cultural beliefs. Aspects of views within a group
28 setting can be distorted, therefore allowing participants to revaluate
29 their own positions. Positivists view truth from interviews. Interviews
30 can distort views and reality. The perspective that interpretation of
31 interviews and document analysis cannot be considered as accurate
32 does recognise the pervasiveness of interpretation throughout the
33 interview process. Interviews are treated as socially structured accounts
34 and this fundamentally impacts the data. As a researcher, it is essential
35 to admit that there is no truth to be found. The most that the researcher
36 can achieve from interviews is that the interviewee answers questions
37 as truthfully and accurately as possible, mirroring his or her
38 understanding, beliefs, feelings and perspectives. Analysis of interview
39 data accordingly has been gathered in a narrative rather than a realistic
40 approach. Interviews are an important method which helps to decipher
41 a more conspicuous understanding of policy documentation. With the

interviews and focus groups, the researcher was able to form an informed decision about the three case study HEIs commitment to widening participation. Exploratory interviews were considered as an important method of obtaining fundamental information from participants. The participants have the knowledge required by the researcher and are able to reflect on the ideas derived from the questions asked by the interviewer. In accordance with the sample selection, the following points were considered:

- All interviews were conducted on the basis of literature review findings and questions were adapted in accordance with widening participation and BME group classifications.

- The student participants were from BME backgrounds.

- Staff participants were selected on the basis of their roles and responsibilities within the three case study HEIs.

- All participants engaged within the research study on a voluntary basis.

The sample selection for the study was not below eight to ten interviews. With regards to the sample size, it is important that theoretical saturation is developed thus confirming that the data actually confirm the analysis of the study. The theoretical saturation for this research has been achieved through the researcher conducting interviews. The findings were then aligned with the research methods applied.

Data Collection

Document analysis and interviews were used to answer questions for this study. The intention was to examine the approaches the three case study HEIs used to interpret the widening participation national policies in terms of BME students and how these three case study HEIs framed institutional widening participation policy at operational level. For a thorough understanding of how the three case study HEIs implemented widening participation for BME students, the following points were essential:

- Implement a thorough analysis of policy documentation

- Interview widening participation managers and BME students

- Interview administrative staff

By analysing documents, this would help to gain greater understanding of how policies were being translated into practical activity.

Document analysis is especially relevant to this study as some documents HEIs produce are aimed at ensuring the HEIs are being seen to be doing the right thing. The policy documentation implemented within the HEIs is passed after considerable consultation. Bernstein's framework model was used to analyse the three case study HEIs. Fundamentally believes that text can be used to create social control and social advantage where necessary. Case study HEI documents should be considered within their social setting. The analysis of policy documentation at institutional level requires to be analysed within the social setting so that it is more apparent in the methods used to convey meaning to individuals. Analysing documents within the HEIs social setting, the researcher can evaluate the influence of the document on individuals. Viewing and analysing documents in this manner allows a cloudless view of how the HEI perceives widening participation in the context of BME students. The view that HEI documentation is a compelling communication tool for HEIs is imperative when analysing approaches to widening participation and BME inclusion.

Interviews were undertaken to ascertain whether or not staff implemented the policy documentation effectively at operational level within the case study HEIs. Interviews enabled the researcher to gain a greater appreciation of document policy and practice. Participants can claim to implement policy documentation. However, at operational level, this may not be the case. By asking specific questions and asking for operational examples, a clearer understanding of the HEIs widening participation work can be concluded. Interviews were fundamentally essential for providing more freedom to probe policy documentation. Using interviews helped in understanding points raised within policy documentation and the framing of practices implemented within the case study HEIs. Semi-structured interviews were chosen as they were considered to be far more flexible. The three case study HEIs were considered different in their approaches to widening participation and inclusion of BME students; therefore, a rigidly structured set of questions would have limited input.

Interviews allow for a detailed explanation from the participants' perspective. Interviews are clearly focused around socially structured accounts, providing the researcher with clear and informed detail,

1 therefore allowing the researcher to appreciate and understand the data.
2 Referring back to the aim of the study, it is imperative to understand
3 how the three case study HEIs interpret the national widening
4 participation policy documentation in particular for BME students.
5 The researcher concentrated on analysing the following areas:

6 • Gain a greater understanding of the HEI policy documentation

7 • Interview widening participation managers, staff in admissions,
8 students in order to formulate an understanding of widening
9 participation policies in practice at the institutional level

10 • Analyse institutional policy documentation with a view to
11 addressing the efficacy of widening participation within HEIs

12 • With the widening participation policies at institutional level a
13 number of fundamental documents were extensively examined
14 in order to understand how the case study HEIs positioned
15 themselves in terms of their policies, the documents are
16 outlined below:

17 • Institutional framework on widening participation

18 • Access agreements

19 • Existing widening participation policies

20 • Admissions policies

21 • Institutional mission statements

22 • Institutional strategic plans for reference related to widening
23 participation

24 Information on the operational aspect of widening participation
25 was achieved through interviews with staff and students. The
26 document analysis was initiated by analysis of Bernstein's framework
27 model. Bernstein's literature features the concept that social meaning
28 is resisted where there is a concern over the balance of power
29 (Bernstein, 2015). The analysis of institutional policy documentation
30 was initiated before interviews were carried out with staff and students,
31 this was viewed as a more sensible method as the researcher could gain
32 a detailed comprehension of the information outlined within the
33 widening participation documentation. A more realistic account can be
34 achieved by analysing, who, why and what has brought the policy
35 documentation into existence. For this study, semi-structured

1 interviews were deemed to be most appropriate for the study, as this
2 method allowed for flexibility. The use of semi-structured interviews
3 allowed for considerable flexibility and the potential for depth of
4 analysis and follow up questions. The researcher conducted interviews
5 using three phases. Initially, the overall context of the study was
6 explained and the focus of the study was outlined. Secondly, structured
7 questions were defined. Finally, open questions were put to the
8 participants. The analysis of the data was delivered using the
9 recommended approaches to analysing every single interview. The
10 interviews were paraphrased and categorised under the fundamental
11 research themes outlined in previous chapters.

Focus group interviews

13 The focus group interviews were centred on the fundamental
14 factors of widening participation and BME student experiences. The
15 process involved with focus group interviews commenced with a clear
16 and structured analysis of exploratory interviews (Willis, 2007).

17 Conducting focus group interviews involved in-depth investigations
18 regarding widening participation HEI policy in terms of BME students.
19 It was mandatory that the students selected for the interviews were
20 enrolled on and attending a three-year HEI degree. Members of staff
21 participating in the research study were based at the three HEIs.
22 Participants were derived from a number of different courses within
23 the case study HEIs. Ninety students were interviewed (thirty from
24 each of the case study HEIs) and thirty staff (ten from each of the case
25 study HEIs). The staff participants from each of the case study HEIs
26 were employed as managers and administrative staff. This sample size
27 was derived to ensure that it was extensive. The core structure of the
28 interviews was formulated in relation to the extensive literature review.

Data Analysis

30 Qualitative data analysis allows for meaning to be built from the
31 data set. The conceptual framework set out in the literature review
32 defined the structure of what required to be achieved. The data analysis
33 phase moved through three iterations of analysis. As the researcher was
34 in a novice position, the aim was, therefore, to focus on the data and
35 keep the centrality of the data as paramount. The analysis phase of the
36 research study commenced when the data collection stage was
37 undertaken. Categorising started early on in the data analysis stage.
38 Data reduction follows a continuous process. This was fundamental
39 through to the final stages of the research process and conclusions. On

completion of the data collected initial stages of coding were commenced. Coding is a process which can define and contextualise the data. Categorising then followed; each participant brought their own experiences and views. The difficulties of working within the boundaries of the coding process, following discussions with the supervisory team the thematic analysis framework was deployed.

Thematic coding allows for mainstream analysis to occur. Thematic analysis was a useful framework to use as it provides key skills and is considered as independent from epistemological theories. The thematic analysis provides a rich and detail analysis of the data. The structural process of thematic analysis is based around six fundamental concepts outlined below:

- Familiarity of data

- Initial code generation

- Selecting themes

- Reviewing themes

- Defining themes

- Producing the report element

Participants' themes and subthemes were outlined as part of point three and four. The thematic analysis allows the researcher to identify fundamental concerns within HEIs but further to this allows for the sharing of issues and understanding of social justice. Fundamental themes have been outlined in previous chapters. Interviews were carried out with thirty members of staff – ten staff per HEI. Ninety students were interviewed through focus group interviews, which involved thirty students per HEI. The interviews were then transcribed and manually input using Excel software. Complete answers were analysed using coding and code links outlined. Once each transcript was put together, the codes and code families were printed as this allowed for differences and familiarities to be clearly viewed. The use of coding does lead to a rigid and systematic approach to data analysed.

Ethical considerations

Research ethics are essential to address moral concerns, ethical consideration is seen as essential to address and consider potential concerns arising from the research and therefore, is required to strengthen ethical consideration. Ethical consideration is required to

1 address the dilemmas that may arise through the research study.
2 Research ethics are essentially concerned with participants and the
3 researcher, in essence, ensuring that positive outcomes can arise for
4 both the researcher and the participants. Researchers are, therefore, in
5 a position to decide on which aspect of ethical principles apply to their
6 research study (Wiles, 2013).

7 The legality within ethics defines the boundaries that the research
8 must be limited to and act within, ethical regulations and professional
9 guidelines are required to be addressed at all times, and decision making
10 should be based on these guidelines, Wiles (2013). Ethical frameworks
11 influence decision making. Common five approaches deployed
12 through (Wiles, 2013)

13 • Consequentialist

14 • Non-consequentialist

15 • Principlist

16 • Ethics of care

17 • Virtue ethics

18 The consequentialist framework emphasises positive outcomes,
19 despite individual views. For example, when considering wider society,
20 for this study, it was important to look at the wider society and the
21 influences on students (Wiles, 2013). A non- consequentialist
22 framework, views moral actions to be above and beyond wider society,
23 in essence for this study how the actions of staff within the case study
24 HEIs have an impact on BME students (Wiles, 2013). Participant
25 confidences are honoured regardless of any benefit to the researcher,
26 the researcher has consistently followed this point throughout and after
27 the study has been completed. Principlists falls into the category of
28 non-consequentialism, allowing for the principles of respect to guide
29 ethical decision making, therefore following the principles of:

30 • Autonomy

31 • Participants volunteering

32 • Gaining informed consent

33 • Ensuring confidentiality

34 • Ensuring anonymity

- Beneficence – Responsibility to do good

- Non-maleficence- avoiding harm

- Justice – benefit of the study

Priority was given to principles where conflict occurs within the study, however, the principlist approach will be followed throughout to ensure consent was obtained from the participants for this study. The ethics of care focuses on the care and compassion that will benefit participants; this has been consistently followed through throughout the study. Virtue ethics involves basing the ethics as person-based approach, where the integrity of the research is fundamental. Participant respect involves considerations of the responsibility to do as good as the beneficence states and avoid any harm which involves the non-maleficence. Questions which were required to be addressed by the researcher are outlined below:

- What are the beneficial consequences of the research study?

- How can informed consent be obtained from participants?

- How is confidentiality of participants protected?

- What are the consequences of the study for participants?

- How will the researcher's role impact on the study?

    (Brinkmann, 2012, p.52-53)

The questions outlined in the research need to be addressed, ethical commitment is essential in developing and formulating research strategies. Ethical considerations have been addressed within this research. The notion that participants should be respected at all times and protected from harm that could arise as a result of the research. For this study, the researcher considered all ethical guidelines before carrying out the study. Participants were given full details of the research study and informed consent was obtained from participants. A letter and consent form was given to volunteers within the three case study HEIs. The letter outlined the purpose of the study, outlining that participation was voluntary and participants were informed that information regarding their participation was not going to be identifiable. Following ethical guidelines and addressing ethical considerations for the study were essentially in place before the research study was approached. Ethical approval was obtained from the ethics committee. The ethics of care framework as set out above have been followed for this small scale research study. As human participants were required for this study, a proposal was put together for ethical approval through the university. Ethical considerations were further widened in order to support the variety of participants involved in the study.

The research did not have any implications on participant workload which was considered essential for staff and students participating in the study. Interviews were scheduled for one hour in order to minimise disruption. The guidelines set out by the British Educational Research Association stipulates that participants should be free to withdraw from the research study at any point – this was made clear to participants from the start of the research study. Participants were informed that they could refuse to answer any questions they felt uncomfortable answering. The three case study HEIs were given pseudonyms in order to ensure anonymity. Within the principalist framework beneficence requires that harm is minimised in the research study (Wiles, 2013). Written consent was essential for participants to complete as this would establish participant's full consent to be part of the research study. The research process was outlined in detail for all participants and this process was completed on an individual basis. The consent form made clear what the research project entailed and what involvement the participants would have in the process. Data obtained from participants would be kept confidential and anonymity provided for each participant. Researcher and participant to the research study make the relationship between both integral to the research study. Both the researcher and the participants need to be fully immersed in the research study particularly where personal experiences are being investigated. Participants are the main providers of data obtained by the researcher. As stated in previous sections, it is the responsibility of the researcher to ensure that participants feel welcome, in a non-threatening environment whereby the participants are feeling comfortable in the process of sharing their experiences and personal views. This non-threatening environment highlights the concept of the researcher being empathetic towards participants. By creating a non-threatening environment, participants are more inclined to immerse themselves within the study.

With the openness and informal welcoming environment, the researcher and participants feel far more intimate, within an informal and non-hierarchical atmosphere. This, in effect, allows for the creation of power equality. There is the concern that qualitative research inquiry impacts on the power relationship balance between the researcher and

1   participant. The researcher for this study followed the constructivist
2   methodological approach, whereby the balance of power between the
3   researcher and the participants created an environment of
4   understanding. It is critical to point out here that the relationship
5   between the researcher and the participants changes in accordance with
6   researcher personality traits, social, cultural backgrounds, perceptions
7   the researcher has developed through the researcher role and
8   responsibility. As a female practitioner and from a BME background,
9   it was imperative that the researcher's own perceptions and conclusions
10   did not impact on participant responses. Hierarchical positioning was
11   deemed fundamental to ensure that the researcher did not create a
12   power in-balance ensuring that an expert subject relationship was
13   developed. With this study, the relationships between the researcher
14   and the participants are considered as highly hierarchical as the
15   researcher endeavours not to influence participants within the
16   interview sessions. Ethically relationships between the researcher and
17   the participants within this study have been impacted upon in the
18   context of participant personal motivations, and the researcher's
19   requirement to obtain data. The researcher did find that the power
20   balance between the researcher and participant changed through the
21   different stages of the research processes (Wiles (2013) (See Figure 7).

22   **Figure 7.** Power Balance Between Researcher and Participant

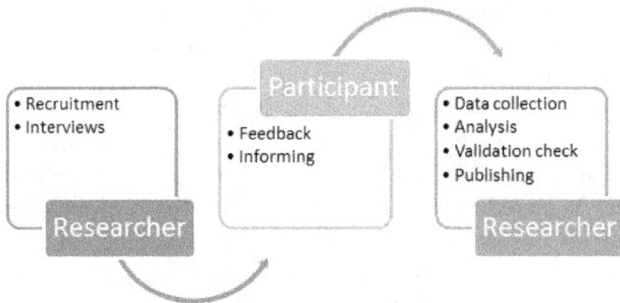

23

24   Qualitative research develops paradoxical ethical dilemmas which
25   present concerns relating to informed consent, confidentiality, social
26   justice, practitioner research (Wiles, 2013). Power relationships within
27   the realms of qualitative research have been addressed through
28   ensuring that real research is advanced (Wiles, 2013). For this study, the
29   power relations between the researcher and participants has changed
30   and passed through different stages as the research study was carried
31   out; this is depicted in Figure 7. The changes in power relations have
32   posed significant ethical dilemmas for the researcher. The researcher

has outlined five fundamental stages which have had an impact on the power balance:

- Initial stages of the research/participant recruitment

- Data collection

- Data analysis

- Validation

- Publishing

The initial stage of the research is considered to be driven by the researcher, whereby the decision of the introduction, goal setting lie with the researcher (Wiles, 2013). The target here is to persuade the participants to be involved in the study, and share their views. As the researcher is in control of the information and the participants are in possession of knowledge and experience are able to use their powers to complete the study (Wiles, 2013). In this study, the researcher found the power balance change as a result of wishing to gain information from the participants. Data collection is where the researcher felt completely dependent on the participant. Control and ownership of the information are in the hands of the participants. Here the researcher aimed to gain considerable information from the participants by asking probing questions. This process was achieved by the researcher by building rapport with the participants. Building rapport does cause ethical concerns, particularly in the methods used to obtain data from the participants. The warm, caring environment the researcher created can be considered as misleading for the participants as this will conceal the true nature of the dialogue (Wiles, 2013). The researcher was aware of the power balance within the interviews, as the interviewer initiated the interview, decided on the topics that were discussed and controlled the interview timings.

However, the researcher was aware of the power of the participants, as participants can determine the levels of engagement within the interview process. During this study, to gain access to participant experiences and understanding, the researcher felt that there was a need to enhance the sense of rapport with the participants. The researcher had to build a considerate and sympathetic relationship and a feeling of trust. The data analysis stage is where the researcher felt that power and control moved back to the researcher. The researcher becomes the storyteller at this stage, the control with the researcher lies in the interpretation of the data obtained; the researcher felt that here ethical

1 considerations were seen as essential. The researcher for this study
2 chose not to ask the participants to comment on the transcripts as they
3 may have led to participants' negative response to findings. The
4 researcher felt that allowing participants to comment on findings may
5 not allow for the preservation of anonymity. It is considered the ethical
6 responsibility of the researcher to ensure that subjects remain
7 anonymous throughout the study (Wiles, 2013). The researcher has felt
8 that the balance of power between interviewer and participant changed
9 throughout the interview process. The researcher believed that the
10 presentation of an honest and clear account of the research was
11 presented to all participants. The researcher followed the principles of
12 clearly explaining the analysis of the data and how this relies on what
13 has been said in the interviews, how it was said and when it was said.
14 The researcher did feel that the interviewer role became inseparable
15 from the research.

16 The researcher had an obligation of protecting professional ethics
17 and respecting participants, before the research was undertaken the
18 goals and the main reasons for the study were outlined. The protection
19 of privacy and anonymity were fundamental to the ethical responsibility
20 of the researcher. The researcher further showed awareness of the
21 developing power relation within the interview environment. The
22 researcher did address fundamental ethical considerations, for example,
23 confirming participant commitment and understanding of the research
24 study, tailoring the language to the participants' understanding,
25 providing participants with reminders. After the study, the researcher
26 ensured that all participant information was anonymous and
27 confidential. Further to this, the researcher ensured that personal
28 values and norms with consideration to institutional pressures were
29 minimised when analysing and interpreting the data.

30 ## Confidentiality

31 Confidentiality was addressed through the use of the informed
32 consent process. Although permission was obtained from participants,
33 they were provided with anonymity to ensure confidentiality. The
34 participants were fully aware of the research study being undertaken.
35 Confidentiality is defined as an explicit or implied guarantee by the
36 researcher to participants within social science research whereby the
37 participants are confident that any information provided to the
38 researcher will not be attributed back to that participant, adapted from
39 (Cresswell, 1998). The assurance of confidentiality carries with it the
40 additional implication that non-researchers will not discover the

1 participant's identity (Cresswell, 1998). Confidentiality is an active
2 attempt by researchers to remove any trace of participant identities
3 from records (Wiles, 2007). There are two types of confidentiality:
4 firstly, explicit confidentiality involves instances whereby the researcher
5 provides a verbal or written specification of the participant's level of
6 confidentiality (Wiles, 2007). In this case, the researcher clearly defines
7 and delineates responsibilities to the participant, and informs the
8 participant of the measures taken to assure the promised level of
9 confidentiality (Allen, 1997).

10   This type of confidentiality is openly negotiated between the
11 researcher and participant and may involve various levels of disclosure,
12 which range from complete disclosure to absolute protection of
13 identity. The essential issue in explicit confidentiality is that
14 expectations and guarantees are clearly elaborated to the participant
15 before the research takes place, and those promises are honoured
16 throughout the research and publication of results. The second type of
17 confidentiality is more difficult to identify. Implied confidentiality
18 involves instances where the researcher implies through either word or
19 deed that the participant's identity and responses are protected. While
20 the researcher may or may not be aware of the implied confidentiality,
21 the researcher becomes responsible for upholding that implied
22 agreement. Implied confidentiality also may involve an unspoken
23 assumption by the participant that the researcher's comments and
24 replies will be un-attributable or off the record. This is particularly
25 problematic when dealing with people who have previously
26 participated in social science research projects where confidentiality
27 was assured. The participant carries expectations and agreements from
28 the previous research into the current project, meanwhile failing to
29 verbalise them to the researcher. Hence, the participant proceeds with
30 the revelation of the information under assumptions of confidentiality
31 with which the researcher is neither familiar nor prepared to honour.
32 This lack of expressed understanding is a common source of conflict
33 between researcher and participant. It is extremely important in most
34 contexts that researchers and participants openly discuss and agree
35 upon the levels of desired confidentiality, thus eliminating any
36 incongruence between participant and researcher expectations. There
37 are several practical issues involved with confidentially (Hopkins,
38 1993). First, there is the ethical responsibility to the people from whom
39 information is gathered. This is because social science examines the
40 public and private lives of people, including their ideas, beliefs,
41 opinions, emotions and attitudes. With this examination comes an

extraordinary level of the potential risk to the people being studied. A participant in a survey or interview may experience social sanctions, peer and family scorn, social controls or any number of other detrimental consequences if the research views are disclosed. Social science carries with it potentially immense risks for participants, social scientists are obligated to conduct their activities within a defined code of conduct which minimizes those risks.

The most critical method for reducing the risks to participants is the protection of the participant's rights, privacy and welfare through an assurance of confidentiality. For this study, the researcher was mindful of participant confidentiality in terms of ensuring risks were eliminated in order to provide participants with reduced risk as stated through. Similarly, the assurance of confidentiality has practical benefits to this study. With an explicit level of confidentiality, the participant is much more likely to participate in a study. Participants are much more likely to give honest and valid responses to questions. The deliberate removal of data, or the production of misleading and dishonest answers, is a distinct possibility if the participant perceives lack of confidentiality and therefore assumes an increased level of risk. Another common phenomenon is the reproduction of publicly acceptable answers. For example, participants who perceive the threat of disclosure of responses or identity are likely to provide data that conform to peer-expectations and general public attitudes, therefore minimising any associated risk. Hence, confidentiality both protects the participant and assures the honesty and the validity of her response. A second issue involves an ethical responsibility toward other researchers. The boundaries of accepted method and ethics have been negotiated, tested and agreed upon over time by scholars with a personal stake in perpetuating their profession. Similarly, those methods and ethics have been refined through peer review and experience dating over the past two centuries.

In the context of confidentiality, the accumulated body of knowledge and experience in the various social science disciplines verifies that confidentiality is an essential component of social science research. Social science research is conducted outside of these boundaries the researcher risks contaminating the research population for all subsequent researchers. For example, if the researcher does not adequately protect the participant's identity in a survey concerning the research and the participant then suffers discrimination based upon revealed identity or responses, that person will most likely be reticent to participate in any future research. Furthermore, if the participant

1 belongs to an organization or community of like-minded individuals,
2 the chances are very high that the organisation will similarly be
3 contaminated and less likely to participate in future research.

4   A third issue that is increasing in importance is the legal liability that
5 comes from conducting social science research. The courts have
6 interpreted the social exchange between researcher and participant as a
7 type of contract that carries with it certain legitimate expectations.
8 Confidentiality is one of these expectations, and confidential
9 participation should not carry intended or unintended penalties for the
10 participant. Participants in social science research have come to expect
11 that their participation should not harm them. The central point here
12 is in assuring that participation in social science research does not
13 penalise the participants' confidentiality. In summary, there are myriad
14 issues surrounding confidentiality; confidentiality is an essential part of
15 social science research. Confidentiality provides an assurance of
16 protection to participants, minimises or eliminates their risk of
17 participation, and involves the active effort of researchers to remove
18 any trace of participant identity from the data. Consequently, students
19 and HEIs should assume that all responses are strictly and completely
20 confidential unless stipulated otherwise, ensuring that active measures
21 are used to eliminate any trace of participant or subject identity from
22 the results.

23   Finally, they should assume all participants in social science
24 research, whether actively or passively involved in providing
25 information to the research, would enjoy and expect confidentiality
26 unless clearly stipulated otherwise. For ethical reasons, students and
27 HEIs should be cautious on the side of caution in clarifying
28 confidentiality with all the sources of data. Maintaining this code of
29 conduct is more difficult and time consuming, however, failing to do
30 this is irresponsible and unethical.

31 ## Research approach summarised

32   As outlined in chapter one and three, this study involved
33 participants, valuing them as individuals with the focus on duty of care.
34 The researcher draws on the human-centred approach for this study,
35 ensuring that integrity and moral duty is at the forefront of this study.
36 The qualitative research approach followed is justified in this section.
37 The theoretical framework is set, and alternative strategies, methods
38 and justification for the chosen methods are outlined. Through an
39 extensive literature review, discussions with supervisors and the
40 mapping out approaches, the research questions for this study were

1 narrowed down. From the initial literature review carried out
2 Bernstein's framework model was investigated and further the concept
3 of critical race theory within HEIs was considered. Fundamental
4 literature for this study was outlined and presented as a move towards
5 the justification for the chosen methodology.

6 This chapter has outlined the research methodology and design
7 followed for this study. The methodological approach applied for this
8 study is based on qualitative research analysis. Validity was ensured by
9 using triangulation and this approach was used throughout the study.
10 The aim of this chapter was to provide a detailed analysis of the
11 methodological framework model used throughout the study. This
12 chapter justified the research decisions undertaken. The purpose of the
13 chapter was to clarify the reasoning behind why the research decisions
14 were undertaken and whether the chosen method was appropriate for
15 the study. The next chapter looks at a detailed analysis of findings, and
16 is based around the researcher's development of the social inclusion
17 framework model.

18

CHAPTER 4

ACADEMIC ATTAINMENT

The author clearly ascertains the perspective that academic achievements of BME students are considerably lower and have not shown any immediate improvements within HEIs (Johnson-Ahorlu, 2017). The impact of this negativity within HEIs towards BME students begins the stereotyping of BME students who no longer feel that they have a voice within society let alone the HEI environment (Hawkins, Carter-Francique, & Cooper, 2016). There is certainly a persistent problem of racism evident within HEIs which has a tremendous impact on social inclusion for BME students. This further exacerbates and complicates BME student academic attainment (Lee, Harrell, Villarreal, & White, 2020).

Through the lens of the CRT theorists, this is just another reminder that racism is active within HEI environments and functions at a level that is often invisible to the eye but prevalent to say the least (Ladson-Billings, 2009). Thus, the theory of CRT endeavours to help society to understand how racism works, and theorist signify that there is a long way to go to address the intractable problem of race within society and in particular HEIs. Moreover, CRT theorists would like to emphasise the fact that issues of race and class must take a central role in knowledge base and practices so that educational leadership is not solely rooted in technical knowledge of leadership and organisational theory but rests in the nuances of creating an HEI environment that works for all students, families and members of the community (Matsuda, 2018). The author has tried to outline the concepts and theorisation of critical race theory in relation to BME students within HEIs in an attempt to bring attention to the fundamental underpinning of how race is used to set racial constraints within HEIs (Mattews, 2019).

Race and Racism

Race and racism are undoubtedly the core elements which are aligned to BME attainment gap. It is interesting to point out here that racism as a term in itself states that there is a fundamental belief that some races are depicted as being better than others based on the colour of their skin (Ogbonnaya-Ogburu, Smith, To, & Toyama, 2020). HEIs are inherently institutionally racist. There is a belief of a superiority attached to HEIs, and as a result, there is a notion that ignorance and dominance are allowed to foster and grow within HEIs (Barnes, 2016). In the UK, BME students make up at least 16% of the total student population, with this percentage varying across HEIs (Patton, 2016). The relationship between income generation and recruitment within HEIs plays an important role in the financial health of the Higher Education sector representing almost a third of the total fees income for HEIs and colleges in the UK (Graham, et al., 2019).

A race crime is any incident that is perceived to be racist by the victim which is motivated by prejudice or hostility against the victims to be motivated by prejudice or hostility against the victims race or perceived race (Chang, 2020).

Religiously aggravated crime was introduced as a category in 2001. In an era of growing tension between Islam and the West#, this is an important distinction, though there is often overlap, this was seen in a series of attacks on Muslim students at City University in Central London (Gillborn, 2020). The attacks were motivated by both racial and religious hatred. Racially motivated incidents represent 12% of all crime against BME people. It is interesting under the current climate that BMEs are six times as more likely to be stopped and searched than their White counterparts (Huber, Gonzalez, & Solorzano, 2018). Moreover, it is the ethical duty of HEIs to work to protect the BME students to ensure fairness of opportunity (Matsuda, 2018). It is typically subtle in the way that racism manifests itself. Racial stereotypes and their effects have a considerable impact on BME students within HEIs. As previously mentioned, CRT plays a fundamental role in race and racism. Despite there being a number of attempts to address racial inequality, for example, the Race Relations Amendment Act (2000) allied with the Equality and Diversity Act (2010) and the Government UK Higher Education White Paper which was aimed to promote equality of opportunity throughout HEIs and are aimed to promote fairness and equality in HEIs including assessment, learning and teaching which includes curriculum design. Figure 8 clearly articulates the notion that there are racial micro-aggressions embedded within HEIs. The racial and social climate set within HEIs is counterproductive in that, on the one hand, the government is asking HEIs to become inclusive institutions and on the contrary, this is quite difficult with the number of micro-aggressions occurring within the institutions at every level of the HEI student

1   experience.

2   **Figure 8.** Racial and social climate for BME students

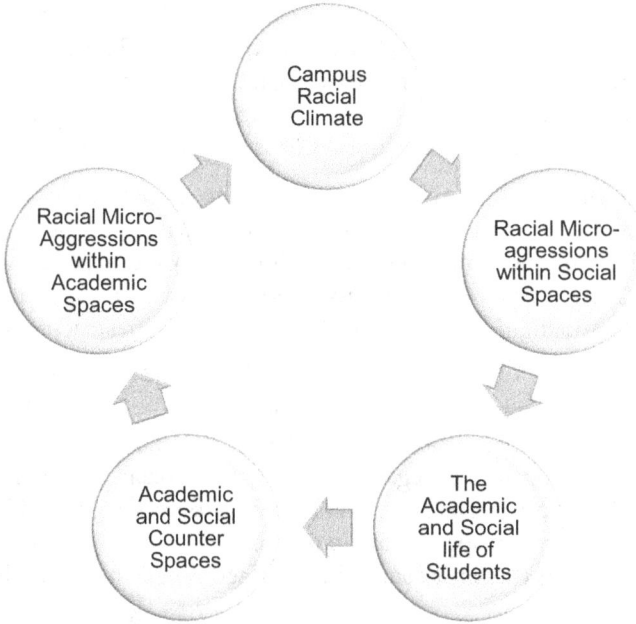

3

4   Moreover, it is the responsibility of HEIs to adhere to government
5   policies and work with the Office For Fair Access (OFFA) in order to
6   promote fairness within HEIs in particular toward low or under-
7   represented groups (Bradbury, 2020). In essence, racial micro-
8   aggressions take a number of forms which consist of verbal and non-
9   verbal assumptions about the lowered expectations academics have
10   towards BME students. The racial and social climate for BEM students
11   depicted in figure 8 suggests that BME students struggle to feel
12   accepted throughout University life (Rollock & Dixson, 2016) (Sablan,
13   2019). BME students are fundamentally undermined within academia,
14   and as a result, they are instilled with self-doubt and engrained with the
15   belief that they are low achievers. Racial segregation is evident among
16   in-class study groups and that of their peers (Zhu, Peng, & Qui, 2019).
17   BME students feel diminished by non-verbal micro-aggressions.
18   Stereotyping BMEs creates negative assumptions about BMEs, where
19   figure 8 clearly shows the continuous circle (Parker, 2019). BME
20   students have a belief that lecturing staff and White students have lower
21   expectations of them. Therefore there is a self-fulfilling prophesy of
22   negativity in terms of their experiences throughout their University

1   experience (Stovall, 2016). The collegiate racial climate fosters more
2   covert and subtle racism within academic spaces and more overt racism
3   within social spaces on campus (Polite & Santiago, 2017). Racial micro-
4   aggressions and negative impact on social spaces have a tremendous
5   consequence on BME students (Trazo & Kim, 2019). The experiences
6   of BME students demonstrates that regardless of accomplishments
7   where educational conditions superficially appear equal, inequality and
8   discrimination exist in subtle, hidden forms (Barnes, 2016).

9   The author analysed widening participation documentation in all
10   three HEIs based on the notion that race and racism are the product
11   of social thought and power relations (Moodley, Mujtaba, & Kleiman,
12   2017). CRT theorists endeavour to expose the way in which racial
13   inequality is maintained through the operation of structures and
14   assumptions that appear normal and unremarkable (Su, 2017).

15   CRT theorists who have a much longer history in the USA is
16   grounded in the uncompromising insistence that race should occupy
17   the central position in any legal, educational or social policy analysis
18   (Patton, 2016). Anti-racists have made some progress in the UK after
19   years of establishment opposition, in making anti-racism a mainstream
20   rallying point, and this is reflected in the Race Relations Amendment
21   Act (2000).

22

CHAPTER 5

BLACK MINORITY ETHNIC EXPERIENCES

This chapter encompasses the experiences of BME students within HEIs. Through the research study carried out by the author, there were several findings which illustrated the issues surrounding BME students within HEIs (Daftary, 2018). Although BME students in the UK are visibly engaging within their studies, it is very evident through feedback that there is a considerable attainment gap between BME students and their White counterparts (Adams, 2017). The authors study clearly illustrated that there is an inconsistency in the approach of the teaching, learning and assessment strategy which HEIs have incorporated within the curriculum. There is considerable differentiation within HEIs which tend to have a higher rate of widening participation students (Goessling, 2018).

Additionally, to this it is noted through the research carried out by the author that teaching staff encountered numerous obstacles when trying to address widening participation student teaching, learning and assessment (Polite & Santiago, 2017). HEIs teaching staff struggled with the methods and approaches that were necessary to ensure the engagement of BME students (Graham, et al., 2019). Although HEIs are constantly trying to understand how to engage and implement change for BME students the lack of clear engagement between BME students and staff is quite implicit within the negative attributes associated with the notion of student engagement and attainment for BME students (Moschel, 2019). This lack of dialogue between individuals and organisations suggest a complicit acceptance, tolerance and even support of institutional and individual racism within HEIs (Mattews, 2019). The author believes that considerable work is to be carried out in unpacking and addressing the educational realities of those who are economically, socially and politically underserved and oppressed by implicit and overt racism (Sleeter, 2017).

It was outlined clearly that mis-education, mis-labelling and mistreatment based on race often develops at a very young age, and this is followed through to their further and higher-level study (Walls, 2016). It was noted that change within HEIs is difficult and will require systematic strategic planning and the mobilisation of key resources

1 (Mensah, 2019). Given the level of historic controversy and enmity
2 about these concerns, the challenge to create a more just system in HEI
3 education is significant (Mattews, 2019). HEIs to this date are
4 institutionally inherent with racism and has played a significant role in
5 the underachievement amongst BME students (Lee, Harrell, Villarreal,
6 & White, 2020).

7 Institutional racism and low expectations by academics signify the
8 low attainment of BME students within UK HEIs. Institutional racism
9 has a disproportionately negative impact on BMEs (Gilborn,
10 Warmington, & Denmack, 2018). Moreover, UK HEIs are finding
11 immigration as well as already existing racial and ethnic diversity,
12 posing significant challenges (Mills & Unsworth, 2018). The
13 hierarchical focus on institutional inclusion for BME is
14 disproportionately lower than advocated by government bodies.
15 Support mechanism and funding pots to support BME students are
16 also questionable (Richards, Awokoya, Bridges, & Clark, 2018). It has
17 been established through a variety of research contributions that there
18 is a lack of support and guidance coupled with the elitist attitude of
19 teaching staff and peers who are from White middle-class backgrounds
20 (Garcia & Velez, 2018). Institutional racism highlighted in previous
21 sections does raise concerns and takes the form of many guises within
22 HEIs (Daftary, 2018).

23 Several studies carried out show that students who are from BME
24 backgrounds are far more inclined to be rejected on application to
25 HEIs and that there is a degree of discrimination by admission tutors
26 (Johnson-Ahorlu, 2017).

27 The Race Relations Amendment Act (2000) emphasises the
28 requirement by public authorities to develop clear race equality
29 strategies and limit unlawful discrimination towards individuals from
30 BME backgrounds (Kennedy, 2017). The particular focus of the Race
31 Relations Amendment Act (2000) is to ensure policies and practices
32 within HEIs are followed clearly (Ogbonnaya-Ogburu, Smith, To, &
33 Toyama, 2020). BME students should be encouraged to target
34 monitoring, assessment and review policies within their HEIs and
35 ensure Race and Equality policies and practice are adhered to.

36 ## Social Inclusion and Social Exclusion

37 A socially inclusive society is defined as one where all people are
38 valued; their differences are respected, and their basic needs are met so
39 they can live in dignity. Social inclusion is used to describe the opposite

effect to social exclusion (Anyon, Lechuga, Downing, Greer, & Simmons, 2018). It usually results from positive action taken to change the circumstances and habitats that lead or have led to social exclusion (Ladson-Billings, 2009). Social exclusion defined signifies how particular people have no recognition by or voice or stake in the society which they live in (Sleeter, 2017). The causes of social exclusion are multiple and usually appear connected with factors affecting a persons' or communities' socioeconomic circumstances, where the effect prevents people from participating fully in society. Social exclusion is the process of being shut out from the social, economic, political and cultural systems which contribute to the integration of a person into the community (Rector-Aranda). As a discipline from which to consider the social inclusion and exclusion concepts, sociology offers a clever overview which presents significant research outlining this concept (Howard & Navarro, 2016). Sociology is well oriented to consider facets of social equality and inequality, social integration and stratification, social mobility as it relates to social inclusion and exclusion and the functional contribution of the periphery relative to the social core. Processes of inclusion and exclusion were features of all hierarchies (Huber, Gonzalez, & Solorzano, 2018).

The terms of inclusion and exclusion feed into efforts to define what might be called social ontology, or the way that the existence and social positioning of groups in a hierarchically structured society would be explained (Annamma, Ferri, & Connor, 2018).

Social interconnectivity is as fundamental as most basic human needs for warmth, sustenance and shelter and that the absence of such connectivity is experienced literally as pain (Lee, Harrell, Villarreal, & White, 2020). A sociological perspective might suggest at the societal level that there exists a series of motivations to design inclusive frameworks for the betterment of social life a natural order perspective would suggest that basic human survival and reproduction benefit from the evolution of cohesive group living, that to an extent, inclusion and exclusion as components of an ideographic means may have helped to ensure evolutionary and reproductive fitness (Lee, Harrell, Villarreal, & White, 2020).

This perspective suggests that such fitness at the level of family networks or community groups may mirror existing physiological traits for responding to physical pain, to structure responses to social pain (Walls, 2016). From this perspective, the exclusion and inclusion within the education continuum exist alongside a biologically driven,

1   psychological reaction that leads to the adoption of a generalised dislike
2   of social exclusion and a favouring of the maintenance of adequate
3   inclusion (Singer & Garner, 2017). Stigma and the act off stigmatising
4   are a common and recognisable form of social exclusion, yet efforts to
5   contend with some of the prejudices and discriminations recognised as
6   components of stigmatisation reflect forms of social inclusion.

7   This further identifies the means and ways that inclusion and
8   exclusion are both enacted and talked about. The university application
9   forms and procedures require considerable skill to complete. It is
10   important to note here that non-traditional students struggle to
11   understand the demands and expectations of higher education (Stovall,
12   2018). Key differences faced by non-traditional students, specifically
13   reading and structuring assignments, are not made clear to students
14   from widening participation strategy. Non-traditional students struggle
15   to understand the demands and expectations of higher education
16   (Borrell, 2018). Key differences faced by non-traditional students,
17   specifically reading and structuring assignments, are not made clear to
18   students from widening participation backgrounds.

19   Academic standards are fundamentally criticised on account of
20   misconceptions of understanding. University resources are inaccessible
21   to all but the most academically able as a consequence setting back
22   rather than enhancing student ability (Mattews, 2019). It is believed that
23   the relationship between the non-traditional student and that of the
24   teaching staff within HEIs can be problematic (Blaisdell, 2019). This
25   view is prevalent, particularly where non-traditional students feel
26   inadequate in higher education environments. Widening participation
27   strategies are inadequate in promoting higher education for BME and
28   Widening participation students (James & Russell, 2019). HEIs should
29   show commitment to students from widening participation
30   backgrounds.

31   Furthermore, there is a need to change attitudes and practices.
32   Lecturing staff working in red brick HEIs who aim to enhance social
33   equity and have a concern for social justice tend to find that they are
34   marginalised within their HEIs (Hurtardo, 2019). It can be signified
35   here that lecturers within HEIs are faced with difficult roles where non-
36   traditional students are concerned. It became apparent that student
37   learning is fundamentally their own concern as the academic role is
38   more of a facilitator. Assessment, teaching and learning caused
39   considerable anxiety for BME students (Allen, 2017). University
40   environments are considered as hostile towards non-traditional

1   students.

2   It is believed that academic and administrative staff are more
3   inclined to support students who are from White middle-class
4   backgrounds (Johnson-Ahorlu, 2017). Alienation is a fundamental
5   criterion which widening participation students experience within
6   HEIs. Financial, childcare concerns, academic understanding, HEI
7   documentation, cultural issues, time management concerns expressed
8   by students from widening participation backgrounds are clear issues
9   which HEIs need to address. The view put forward the perspective of
10 financial concerns surrounding students from lower socio-economic
11 backgrounds and those who attend university through widening
12 participation initiatives are coupled with the increased bureaucracy the
13 HEIs force upon them (Mattews, 2019). Correspondingly there is a
14 view that there is a multitude of students from low socio-economic
15 backgrounds do not have a bank account and therefore unable to apply
16 for student loans. Significant research studies clearly define that these
17 cases are further highlighted whereby students from low socio-
18 economic backgrounds do not have resources available to them which
19 do hinder their learning significantly (Perez Huber & Solorzano, 2018).

20 The removal of maintenance grants has exacerbated student
21 poverty forcing students towards paid work and in some cases leaving
22 programmes of study. It is strongly believed that financial hardship
23 developed for BME students is largely due to HEI policies and has very
24 little to do with government initiatives (Kennedy, 2017). Students from
25 widening   participation   backgrounds   have   disproportionate
26 representation. Research carried out by the author further argues that
27 HEIs are significantly charging students a higher fee and are working
28 in line with OFFA.

29 Fundamental factors analysing the concepts of why non-traditional
30 students find entering and remaining in higher education a difficult
31 process is not addressed by government policy documentation (Borrell,
32 2018). HEIs are directly responsible for the limited support
33 mechanisms in place for widening participation students.

34 An important point to note here is that class tendencies are
35 compounded by race. Additional constraints are enforced with family
36 backgrounds and cultural backgrounds (Parker, 2019). There is reduced
37 choice in inclusive learning for BME students which is evident.
38 Widening participation has created a mass influx in higher education.
39 Absence of visible understanding and limited knowledge of cultural
40 diversity fundamentally prevents the widening participation strategies

1 to be workable within HEIs (Richards et al., 2018).

2 There are distinct inequalities in place which essentially are barriers
3 to hostility engaging BME students. There are considerably limited
4 initiatives to address BME student concerns within HEIs (Christian,
5 Seamster, & Ray, 2019). Fundamentally visible inequalities are
6 prevalent within HEIs. Predominately students from BME and
7 widening participation backgrounds require significant encouragement
8 and guidance prior to attending HEIs (Allen, 2017). This will
9 contribute to the motivation and self-esteem of BME students.
10 Predominantly students from BME and widening participation
11 backgrounds require significant encouragement and guidance prior to
12 attending HIEs (Yao, George, & Malaney, 2019). Ethnic minority
13 students will not achieve good degrees as they do not have strong
14 underpinning prior to accessing HEI education.

15 Asian and BME students are less likely to achieve success when
16 entering higher education, as they are not academically prepared
17 (Jackson & Barton, 2017). If teaching staff are more familiar with
18 cultural and social backgrounds of BME students, this would benefit
19 BME widening participation students immensely (Mattews, 2019).
20 Interestingly there is much discussion on the view that financial
21 situations, friendships and university support are fundamental areas
22 which addressed correctly would encourage students from BME and
23 widening participation backgrounds to succeed (Mensah, 2019).

24 It is arguably believed that there should be a sense of belonging and
25 cultural understanding which would at least allow BME students to
26 continue with their studies. Students who attend University from the
27 non-traditional backgrounds are overwhelmed by the sheer size of the
28 groups, particularly within lecture theatres and accordingly are unable
29 to engage in university life. Essentially, this impacts on the recruitment
30 and retention of BME students (James & Russell, 2019).

31 Experiences outlined in previous sections play an essential part in
32 the lack of engagement from minority groups (Moodley, Mujtaba, &
33 Kleiman, 2017). The epistemological, social and pedagogical challenges
34 faced by BME students have a direct consequence on the teaching,
35 learning and assessment of these students (Mensah, 2019). The removal
36 of external concerns highlighted in previous sections will allow for the
37 improvement of BME student experiences.

38 There are a number of obstacles associated with the movement of
39 students from further education HEIs. Concerns relating to social class

and the absence of attention and guidance provided to teaching staff has resulted in social class and absence of attention and guidance provided to teaching staff (Kennedy, 2017). Concerns related to social class and the absence of attention and guidance provided to teaching staff has resulted in negative learning experiences for BME students.

It is argued that institutional culture does not address cultural diversity (Bimper, 2017). Social inclusion for BME students is inclined to be supported by parental pressures. Family pressures and influences are fundamental factors to promote social inclusion in HEIs. Student experiences which are formed from further education teaching, learning and assessment conceptualisation find extensive challenges in transferring to HEIs and many non-traditional student groups find themselves alienated and unable to cope with the demands of HEIs (Howard & Navarro, 2016).

Inadequate support mechanisms and a limited sense of institutional belonging add to the difficulties associated with social inclusion. Attempts have been made to address concerns of social inclusion, however, students studying foundation degrees and then topping up to a degree status within HEIs allow for a greater progression and completion. BME students are far more highly represented in contrast to their White middle-class counterparts, particularly within post-92 HEIs (Lee, Harrell, Villarreal, & White, 2020).

Social Inclusion issues become more apparent within red brick HEIs. It is also interesting to acknowledge that red brick HEIs remain predominantly White middle-class environments (James & Russell, 2019). Social, cultural and economic backgrounds are the fundamental driving forces on whether or not students achieve actual success. Degree courses which are predominantly studied by BME students achieve actual success (Annamma, Ferri, & Connor, 2018).

Despite the introduction of government initiatives to address BME issues within HEIs are admittedly considered as elitist environments tailored for the White middle classes. BME students are highly represented in HEIs, and these students are clustered within post 92 HEIs (Jackson & Barton, 2017).

Diversity and Equality

BME students, in particular those from working class backgrounds, and females with BME backgrounds, do not feel a sense of belonging. BME females feel ostracised and lack a sense of belonging within HEIs (Mensah, 2019). Non-traditional students are also susceptible to

1 withdrawing from courses or not completing courses and are having to
2 resit assessments. Although pre-92 HEIs offer larger bursaries to
3 students from BME backgrounds, fewer BME students and students
4 from poorer backgrounds actually attend these HEIs (Jackson &
5 Barton, 2017). Pre-92 HEIs use widening participation funding and are
6 willing to offer and places from poorer backgrounds and BME students
7 who are essentially high achievers.

8   There is an increase in racial bias when allocating HEI places
9 (Stovall, 2016). Student experience is very different BME students and
10 their White middle-class counterparts. Communication between staff
11 and BME students are deemed insensitive, adding to the hostile
12 environment induced within HEIs. Degree classification for students
13 who are from BME backgrounds is much lower than their White
14 middle-class counterparts (Su, 2017).

15

CHAPTER 6

THE SOCIETAL CURRICULUM

A societal curriculum is the knowledge, ideas, and impressions about ethnic groups that are portrayed in the mass media. Television programs, newspapers, magazines, and movies are much more than mere factual information or idle entertainment (Delgado & Stefancic, 2017). For many students, mass media is the only source of knowledge about ethnic diversity; for others, what is seen on television is more influential and memorable than what is learned from books in classrooms (Gillborn, 2020). Ethnic stereotyping purports that these programs perpetuate myths about life outside of White mainstream UK which contribute to an understanding of minority cultures as less significant and as marginal (Garcia & Velez, 2018). Ethnic distortions in mass media are not limited to news programs; they are pervasive in other types of programming as well (Borrell, 2018). The messages they transmit are too influential for academic to ignore; therefore, culturally responsive teaching includes thorough and critical analyses of how ethnic groups and experiences are presented in mass media and popular culture (Flores, 2017). Academics need to understand how media images of BMEs are manipulated; the effects they have on different ethnic groups; what formal HEI curriculum and instruction can do to counteract their influences; and how to teach students to be discerning consumers of and resisters to ethnic information disseminated through the societal curriculum.

Culturally responsive teaching places academics in an ethical, emotional, and academic partnership with ethnically diverse students, a partnership that is anchored in respect, honour, integrity and resource sharing (Mattews, 2019). In culturally responsive teaching, the "knowledge" of interest is information about BME groups; the "strategic thinking" is how this cultural knowledge is used to redesign and involve students working with each other and with teachers as partners to improve their achievement. Academics need to understand that culturally responsive caring is action-oriented in that it demonstrates high expectations and uses imaginative strategies to ensure academic success for BME students (Mensah, 2019).

Academics need to be able to decipher these codes to teach BME

1 students more effectively. Differences in BME communication styles
2 have many implications for culturally responsive teaching (Moodley,
3 Mujtaba, & Kleiman, 2017). Understanding BME communication
4 styles is necessary to avoid violating the cultural values of ethnically
5 diverse students in instructional communications; to better decipher
6 their intellectual abilities, needs, and competencies; and to teach them
7 style or code-shifting skills so that they can communicate in different
8 ways with different people in different settings for different purposes
9 (Garcia & Velez, 2018). Culture is deeply embedded in any teaching;
10 therefore, teaching BME students has to be multicultural.

11 It is viewed that the internal structure of ethnic learning styles
12 includes at least eight key components which are configured differently
13 for BME groups, for example, preferred content; ways of working
14 through learning tasks; techniques for organising and conveying ideas
15 and thoughts; physical and social settings for task performance;
16 structural arrangements of work, study, and performance space;
17 perceptual stimulation for receiving, processing, and demonstrating
18 comprehension and competence; motivations, incentives, and rewards
19 for learning; and interpersonal interactional styles (Graham, et al.,
20 2019).

21 These dimensions provide different points of entry and emphasis
22 for matching instruction to the learning styles of students from BME
23 groups (Johnson-Ahorlu, 2017). To respond most effectively to them,
24 academics need to know how they are configured for different ethnic
25 groups as well as the patterns of variance that exist within the
26 configurations (Huber, Gonzalez, & Solorzano, 2018). Another
27 powerful way to establish cultural congruity in teaching is integrating
28 ethnic and cultural diversity into the most fundamental and high status
29 aspects of the instructional process on a habitual basis (Borrell, 2018).
30 Academics should learn how to create a multicultural learning
31 environment through formal and informal aspects of the educational
32 process. Further analysis of reveals that a high percentage of
33 instructional time is devoted to giving examples, scenarios, and
34 vignettes to demonstrate how information, principles, concepts, and
35 skills operate in practice (Howard & Navarro, 2016). These make up
36 the pedagogical bridges that connect prior knowledge with new
37 knowledge, the known with the unknown, and abstractions with lived
38 realities (Bimper, 2017). Academics need to develop rich repertoires of
39 multicultural instructional examples to use in teaching BME students
40 (Ladson-Billings, 2009).

1   This is a learned skill that should be taught in academic
2 development skills. The process begins with understanding the role and
3 prominence of examples in the instructional process, knowing the
4 cultures and experiences of different ethnic groups, harvesting teaching
5 examples from these critical sources, and learning how to apply
6 multicultural examples in teaching other knowledge and skills—for
7 instance, using illustrations from BME scholars (Lavender, 2019).

8   Research indicates that culturally relevant examples have positive
9 effects on the academic achievement of BME students. A wide variety
10 of other techniques for incorporating a culturally diverse contribution
11 can be extracted from the work of BME scholars (Delgado & Stefancic,
12 2017). They are valuable models and incentives for doing culturally
13 responsive teaching and should be a routine part of teacher preparation
14 programs. BME culture strongly influences the attitudes and values that
15 students and academics bring to the instructional process.

16   Learning, teaching and assessment for BME students is a major
17 determinant of how the problems of underachievement are solved for
18 BME students (Blaisdell, 2019). To a large extent, HEIs have not been
19 very culturally responsive to BME students. Instead, BME students
20 have been expected to divorce themselves from their cultures and learn
21 according to White middle-class cultural norms. BME students are
22 placed in a difficult academic environment as they are obligated to
23 master the academic tasks while functioning under cultural conditions
24 unnatural and often unfamiliar to them (Goessling, 2018). Removing
25 academic barriers for BME students is a significant contribution to
26 improving their academic achievement.

27   Removing barriers to education for BME students is culturally
28 responsive to BME students throughout their instructional processes
29 (Mattews, 2019). Recruitment and retention Across the UK higher
30 education sector, both continuation rates and completion rates are
31 deemed significantly lower for ethnic minority students (Bimper, 2017).

32   The completion rates of minority students were also found to be
33 considerably lower and varied significantly between minority groups.
34 HEIs with high early leaving rates have a higher than average
35 representation of ethnic minority students (Patton, 2016). The early
36 leaving rate has a significant- association with ethnicity and non-
37 completion. Specifically, Black British and Pakistani Asian British
38 students are found to be significantly more likely to drop-out than
39 White, Indian, Asian, British and Chinese students (Blaisdell, 2019).

BME students believe they fail to grasp the academic concepts in terms of passing assessments which leads them to leave their studies. BME students are more inclined to leave their studies as there is an emphasis on the family and social consequences of failure (Hawkins, Carter-Francique, & Cooper, 2016). The issue of race creates particularly sharp divisions between BME students and their White counterparts, with both Black and White respondents positioning themselves as at risk from issues concerning race (Barnes, 2016). BME students believe that institutional racisms may hinder their chances of success. There is continued domination within HEIs by middle-class Whites, both as staff and students. For BME students, unequal distributions of risk by social class are amplified by race adding dangers of racism and alienation for BME students which has an impact on retention of BME students (Ray, Randolph, Underhill, & Luke, 2017). There is a notion of elitism and unhelpfulness in the context of higher education non-traditional students.

There is a requirement that consistent and informative information should be available where widening participation and inclusive learning is concerned (James & Russell, 2019). The fundamental areas of influence of HEI involvement for students who come from BME and widening participation backgrounds are based around attainment and aspirations (Annamma, Ferri, & Connor, 2018). Internal and external driving forces which allow for the successful application and entry into higher education require differentiation.

Internal considerations focus on the ability, motivation and aspirations based upon support and encouragement. External considerations for HEIs are determined by restrictions and opportunities (Christian, Seamster, & Ray, 2019). The cultural harmony created through multicultural education allows for intercultural, interethnic, intergroup understanding and respect within HEIs and the community. Multicultural education within HEIs in terms of BME students is not designed to rewrite history but rather to correct distortions and inaccuracies.

Multicultural education supporting BMEs is a progressive approach for transforming education that critiques and corrects colour-blind and discriminatory curriculum, practices, and policies in HEIs (Kennedy, 2017). Social inclusion is grounded in ideals of social justice and equity, critical pedagogy, and a dedication to providing educational experiences in which all students reach their full potential becoming socially and culturally aware and responsive citizens. Multicultural-education, acknowledges that HEIs are essential for providing an education that helps to eliminate racial injustices and increase racial harmony (Annamma, Ferri, & Connor, 2018).

For HEIs to become areas for social inclusive learning, all curricula must be analysed to ensure accuracy and completeness. The curriculum must be examined to determine how it is re-cycling and supporting oppressive societal and cultural conditions. HEIs in the UK have been relatively immune from scrutiny regarding the racial and ethnic dynamics of HEIs, which as a result have, by and large, been concealed. Where there was scrutiny, it has been suggested that this has resulted in a 'colour blind' approach (Hallmon, Anaza, Sandoval, & Fernandez, 2020). While such a state of affairs was politically sustainable under conditions where HEIs were only accessed by a small and largely privileged section of the population.

CHAPTER 7

GOVERNMENT STRATEGY

BMEs are less likely to be satisfied with their student experience; more likely to leave early; and are less likely to gain a good Honours degree (Cabrera, 2018). Progression to employment may not be as successful or straightforward for BME graduates as a result of their HEI teaching, learning and assessment experiences. Of possible relevance in relation to this last point, there is clear evidence that students from certain BME groups under-perform in relation to degree attainment on a range of measures compared to White students (Chang, 2020).

Social determinants of lifelong participation in learning involve time, place, gender, family and initial schooling (Flores, 2017). Taking a life course approach, this book looks at barriers facing actual and potential students to participate in education and training from early-life educational experiences through to HEIs specifically in relation to BME students (Chang, 2020). The BME attainment gap, evidence points to a complex range of differently connected factors being at play such as: previous educational experiences; curriculum content and design; teaching, learning and assessment approaches; the learning environment; and direct and indirect racism. As has been previously discussed, the reasons for the disparity in attainment are associated with a range of personal, cultural, institutional and structural factors (Allen, 2017).

BME student to remain within HEIs and the fundamental failure to achieve are overlaid with instances of direct and indirect racism (Blaisdell, 2019). Enabling success for BMEs within HEI environments will require a multi-pronged response. Educational problems and barriers for BME student groups focus on the evidence of those from the BME groups that aim high and succeed (Johnson-Ahorlu, 2017). HEI strategies that have been adopted by BME students, with support from their parents and teachers, to raise expectations and achieve good results are essential (Howard & Navarro, 2016). Some of the key negative factors identified include social deprivation, low social capital, racism and poor self-esteem. Despite the odds, BME students can achieve the highest grades (Giraldo, Huerta, & Solorzano, 2017). Some

1 BME students in the UK spent their summers at Imperial College
2 London argues that, while institutional racism plays a significant role in
3 affecting the attainment of BME students, there are other complex
4 factors related to the internalisation of negative attitudes, identities that
5 can be addressed through the correct pedagogical strategies (Dixson &
6 Rousseau, 2018).

7 Moreover, emphasis on the importance of intellectual rigour is
8 underpinned by caring and reliable support and stimulating physical
9 and cultural pursuits. Evidence suggests that due to low teacher
10 expectations, BME students do not feel intellectually stretched
11 (Daftary, 2018). HEIs need to work with BME students and develop
12 self-efficacy, critical self-reflexivity, resilience and cultural capital.

13 These outcomes are associated with the long established traditions
14 of critical pedagogy. While there are some dangers in focusing attention
15 away from wider institutional practices and social oppression, towards
16 the attitudes of BME students, it is important to challenge the idea of
17 BME as victims only (James & Russell, 2019). The benefit of using
18 high-achieving BME professionals and academic staff as role models
19 and mentors is essential for BME students to view HEIs through
20 different lenses. Developing an inclusive curriculum which supports
21 the retention and success of BME students cannot be understated or
22 devalued.

23 It is essential to value BME student differences within the
24 mainstream curriculum, pedagogy and assessment (Hallmon, Anaza,
25 Sandoval, & Fernandez, 2020). Valuing BME students and addressing
26 diversity in learning, teaching and assessment would involve academics
27 becoming aware of the impact of staff and student diversity on the
28 learning process, and the importance of avoiding stereotypical
29 constructs of BME students as 'non-traditional' students and therefore
30 lacking ability to excel (Delgado & Stefancic, 2017). Although some
31 academics take a narrow view associated primarily with the content of
32 what is taught, others adopt a much broader perspective relating to
33 such things as course design, teaching and learning and assessment
34 methods and strategies, as well as course content and pedagogy
35 (Ladson-Billings, 2009). In addition, in what might be conceptualised
36 as a student-centred approach to curriculum design suggests that all
37 aspects need to be designed in ways that can engage and include the
38 needs, interests and aspirations of all students.

39

CHAPTER 8

THEMATIC ANALYSIS

This chapter examines the findings derived from the primary data collected from the research focus group interviews and the document analysis carried out at national, institutional and operational levels. This chapter focuses on answering the research questions stated in chapter one. This section helps to address the fundamental themes outlined in Figure 1 in terms of critical race theory, recruitment and retention, learning, teaching and assessment, race and racism and social inclusion. This study centres on three case study HEIs and examines how government policy documentation is interpreted at institutional level and how BME issues are addressed at institutional level within the HEIs widening participation policy. Whilst maintaining anonymity, data pertaining to the participants are identified. Thematic analysis is presented in this chapter. The fundamental themes identified within this research are critical race theory, recruitment and retention, learning, teaching and assessment, race and racism and social inclusion. Each theme is summarised at the end to reveal the most relevant findings. Key themes to emerge from this study are outlined in Figure 9. The absence of BME considerations within widening participation strategy at institutional level is significant as observed in the three case study HEIs.

The Positioning

The research study focuses on three HEIs based within the north of England. The barriers to participation for BME students are examined within three case study HEIs which are based in the North of England. The thematic analysis has been divided into the three areas of national, institutional and operational level considerations. The UK higher education system does have a considerable degree of freedom when interpreting the national policy framework.

Figure 9. Institutional Level Thematic Analysis

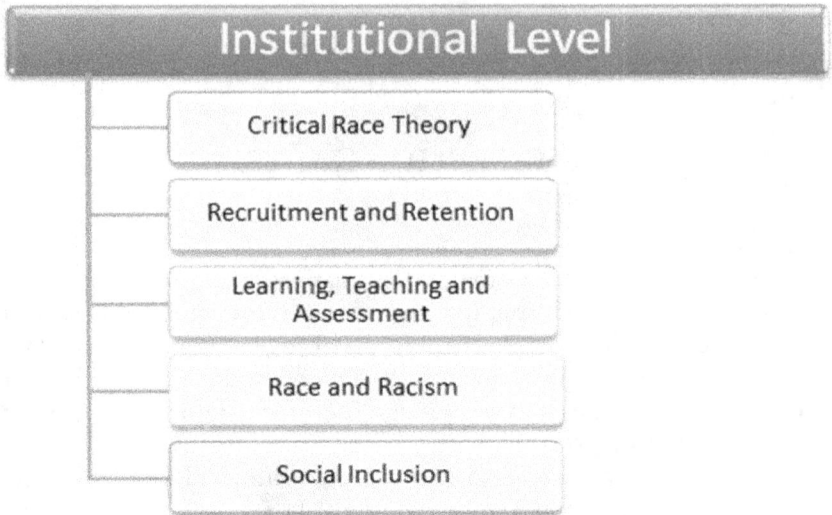

Race and Racism Critical Race Theory

The overall findings from the staff interviews highlighted the complexity and multiplicity of issues relating to BME degree attainment, as well as the inter-sectionality between ethnicity, gender and class as this quote evidences:

> I'm not aware of the details of it all or the size of the gap but I am aware that there is a gap between BME students and White students ... I would imagine that the background factors would play a part, such as kind of first generation people going to university, family pressures, things like that, there'd be a difference in those things for BME students and non-BME students. I think role models would play a part ... it kind of comes from lower down the school system and that kind of plays into it, that their kind of attainment level tracks through, so starting down at a lower level with the social pressures of BME students and to achieve academically or to not achieve academically. (Staff 5 – academic HEI A)

This view reiterates that BME students are not provided with the same level of support throughout their learning. Further to this view of the complications associated with social inclusion are significantly highlighted in the respondent Staff 5 answer outlined above. Across all the HEIs, there was evidence of a strong commitment, at both institutional and grass-roots levels, to widen participation, ensure the equality and diversity of the student body, developing inclusive practices and to enhance belonging.

This was apparent at all levels, strategically and operationally. With regard to students from different cultural backgrounds, there was also a strong commitment to developing cross-cultural interaction. However, much of this awareness and activity relating to inclusivity was generic, relating to all students, and, other than widening participation outreach activity, there was little evidence of interventions designed specifically for BME students. Fewer staff were aware of the actual percentage of BME students studying at their institution, and almost none knew the proportion of BME staff:

> I can't remember the exact percentages for, it's much smaller numbers for black students, I think it's only something like 3%, 4% maybe. I mean White, it's less than 50%, so we do have quite a big mixture of groups plus as I say the largest is British White which is about 45-50%, it varies. Asian but of course because we have this massive intake of Chinese students from overseas and then blacks are about 4%, mixed-race probably 2% and then the other categories similar. Quite low numbers really. (Staff 9 - academic HEI A)

The equality aspect is not being adhered to within HEIs, as is stated by Staff 9. The HEI system is based and designed around the White supremacy. The majority, while knowing that there was an attainment gap across the wider HE sector, were also unable to give any evidence of the gap in their own institution, beyond recognising that, in general, BME students did worse than their White counterparts:

> Um ... I'd have to check the surveys, the module level surveys because I'm not sure of the breakdown. The survey that we carried out ... we probably didn't have ethnicity, I'd have to check. (Staff 1 - academic HEI C)

In some cases, staff did not believe there was a particular gap in their own institution as they were not aware of it:

> We have students from over 130-odd countries and speaking over 40 different languages, it might be just like the culture of the organisation here, that it's very open and people might be thinking about it [attainment gap] in the back of their head or maybe mention it to someone else but it hasn't, as you said,

1   bubbled up to us, because if it actually happens a lot it most
2   likely would bubble up and we'd hear about it but I can't think
3   of anything. (Staff 11 - administrator HEI A)

4   More frequently, staff spoke of other staff being unwilling to discuss
5 issues around ethnic minority students, either for reasons of political
6 correctness" or for fear of saying the wrong thing, meaning that issues
7 of BME under-attainment were being avoided. It was also suggested
8 that such discussions were not taking place within HEIs since formal
9 recognition that there was „a problem" would require HEIs to address
10 it, which would, in turn, incur significant costs – either financial or in
11 relation to staff time. There were, of course, exceptions with some staff
12 being highly aware of the gap and having interrogated their institutional
13 data:

14   I was interested in things like where was the greatest difference?
15   was it early on in the degree?, was it in particular types of
16   coursework, under particular types of assessment mode,
17   between particular sub-groups within the ethnic group? (Staff 8
18   - academic HEI C)

19   The awareness of senior managers regarding their own institutions'
20 attainment gap was patchy. Some were aware of the attainment gap and
21 believed that their plans were in place to address it, although they might
22 not have been directly involved in such discussions since they took
23 place elsewhere within the institution. Other did not believe there was
24 a problem:

25   I mean, I certainly don't think there's much with regards to, you
26   know, black and minority ethnic groups as I say, it's not
27   something that's really discussed in our school or whether it's
28   just something that we think isn't an issue because we think
29   we're dealing with it because we've got all these systems in place
30   that treats everyone fairly and consistently. You know we
31   wouldn't positively discriminate in favour of students we treat
32   them all fairly and equally really so I don't think there's much
33   coming through but I might be wrong. As, I say, the Director of
34   Undergraduate Programmes, she's not aware of anything and
35   the previous Director of Teaching he was never aware of
36   anything. (Staff 8- academic HEI C)

37   Arguably this point is a fundamental concern in inequality. In
38 general, other staff did not believe senior managers were aware of the
39 issues or that there were any institutional strategies designed to address

the gap. From staff 8, there is a belief that not all HEIs are in line with the government's widening participation inclusion. However, while teaching staff also often had little awareness of the gap at institutional level, many were aware of their own course/module attainment breakdown and recognised that there was a gap more locally.

Social Inclusion

Staff understood that some students did do better than others, in terms of retention and success, in essence, this was associated with the systematic, societal inequalities which were based around the social, economic and cultural aspects of social inclusion;

> This is part of a greater social phenomenon that relate to the concept that certain groups whether they are BME or not perform worse than their counterparts, (Staff 13 - academic HEI C)

As HEI C widening participation manager stated:

> Why would you want to keep people out? It does not go well with what higher education is all about. We actually should support students who can complete and access courses.(Staff 13 – academic HEI C)

The widening participation manager at HEI C believed that there should be a greater inclusion of widening participation and that students should be encouraged to attend university. The widening participation manager at HEI A believed that:

> The widening access team which has an inclusive and progressive view does promote the HEI in a positive manner. The language put into the literature does reflect a middle class and traditionally academic culture. It is important for the government to continue the pressures and highlight widening participation as an important agenda. I think HEIs need to respond accordingly to widening participation initiatives. BME is not something we think should be singled out by any means. (Staff 9 – academic HEI A)

BME representation is somewhat inconsistent as outlined by staff 13 and staff 9. Feedback from staff did raise concerns regarding institutional racism militated against BME student success. It was interesting to find that only a minority of staff that HEI's were racist; however, staff did raise the following:

I don't mean that they are racist staff within the HEI, but the
university itself works within set structures which are in essence
for students coming from rich White middle class backgrounds.
These structures don't work with the cohorts that the University
has. (Staff 9 - academic HEI A)

Findings further suggested that pedagogic aspects of social
inclusion were dictated from top down. There were concerns about the
inadequate level of inclusion in concerns with the student body and in
particular White middle class student representation. Staff within all
three case study HEIs were frustrated that they were unable to work
with students from BME backgrounds and felt that trying to initiate
change meant going through significant bureaucracy.

Staff want more rewards and recognition if they are going to
spend more time with ensuring they are working more towards
their teaching and learning and social inclusion. (Staff 4-
academic HEI B)

Some HEI staff within the case study HEIs believed that the
attainment gap between White and BME students was in fact the fault
of the students themselves. This was evident in HEI A that staff were
more research intensive. Areas for concern were associated with
students not having the right academic background, having non-
traditional qualifications coupled with the inadequate knowledge and
the inability to write well academically which was a significant point
raised outlined by staff 9:

They all come in at the same level – but I'm not sure why the
BME student cohort don't really attain well. I don't know if this
is linked to their socio-economic background or their social class
but that tends to be determined by the type of school they have
attended. They will have adopted a certain style…I mean in
terms of their teaching and learning. I don't know if this makes
it more difficult for them to mix? (Staff 9 - academic HEI A)

When they come in on the first day they do a number of
different activities and I tend to seat everyone in alphabetical
order so that there is no prejudice, but when they come back
after their break they have all rearranged themselves into ethnic
groups which is rather worrying. (Staff 4 - academic HEI B)

HEI A the widening participation manager highlighted the
difficulties associated with the national widening participation agenda
and the university's institutional agenda:

1   There are some paths that will not bring candidates to HEIs like
2   HEI A. We appreciate that some disadvantaged groups are more
3   inclined to choose the vocational route. We do, however, try to
4   get these students to move towards other educational options.
5   Sometimes I think we go against what these students need and
6   this doesn't best fit inclusion models. (Staff 7 –academic HEI A)

7   It is essential to understand here that where there is a conflict of
8 interest in terms of the HEI and government national policy when
9 considering widening participation the HEI does move towards
10 watering down their widening participation requirements. The
11 widening participation manager at HEI B argues that social inclusion
12 was clearly addressed within the HEI.

13   Widening participation ensures that social inclusion is a shared
14   commitment by the HEI – it has to be…..we need to have a
15   strong commitment and shared commitment as that is the type
16   of student we are getting. We have to show that we are
17   welcoming these types of students, otherwise, where are we
18   going to get this sort of student from? (Staff 16 – administrator
19   HEI B)

20   In addition to the comments made by staff 16 – HEIs need to be
21 more inclusive as the HEI may not survive as a result of creating social
22 exclusion. Findings suggest that HEIs need to be more inclusive; this
23 was a significant aspect.

24   I can appreciate where HEIs are with this. The point here is that
25   if your department, school call it what you will is recruiting well,
26   what's the point of bothering with widening participation? Why
27   bother when the faculty is taking in people with much better A
28   level results? But where there are BME students we don't really
29   look at making sure our students come from a particular
30   ethnicity…(Staff 15 - academic HEI A)

31   Essentially the viewpoint above emphasises that some HEI staff are
32 not concerned or focused on social inclusion policies and practices.
33 HEI A staff 18 academic:

34   All HEIs are more sympathetic to social inclusion agenda, and
35   these departments are over-subscribed but they are also very
36   much selective. So in terms of your question socially inclusive
37   departments tend to be the science departments, computer
38   science and engineering departments. There are some very
39   passionate individuals out there who believe that social

inclusion, social justice is important, I think social inclusion is really linked more to recruitment, you have to start to think that students want to stay local because of the fees increase for example. (Staff 18 –academic HEI A)

Social inclusion was ignored in many cases for the survival of the HEI. The widening participation managers within the case study HEIs did admit that there were strong overlaps between the recruitment and widening participation work.

I appreciate that HEIs are confused with aspects of social inclusion. The argument here is that if the department you are working in is recruiting well, why would you want to consider widening participation when really you could be getting better 'A' level students? (Staff 19 widening participation manager HEI B). HEI staff should show commitment to students from widening participation backgrounds. Academic staff should enhance social equity.

I think that like all HEIs departments that are finding it harder to recruit will look at widening participation in a different light, whereas departments that are doing very well and are oversubscribed will tend to be more selective. You should be more pragmatic with this. There are some very passionate individuals who are very much focused on BME and widening participation concerns, with social inclusion, social justice and so on and are champions for the cause in terms of motivation for their engagement I think this is a little variable and I think to some it is linked more to recruitment but you have to start thinking that more students are likely to be staying local, so social inclusion needs to be based on what is going on locally even though the institution itself is a national recruiter. (Staff 3 - widening participation manager HEI A)

For some courses case study HEI A did not accept vocational courses at all:

The large concern we have as a Russell Group institution is that our performance indicators and benchmarks, they are based on the tariff and what we don't seem to be doing is basing decisions on tariff points, so what tends to happen is that lots of students may have the tariff points so social inclusion and bringing in students from widening participation backgrounds just doesn't work for us. (Staff 3 – widening participation manager HEI A)

The statement made by the widening participation manager at HEI A illustrates clearly how a large group of students from under-represented groups who have alternative qualifications are not considered by Russell Group HEIs. Findings again suggested that HEI staff fail to address BME student concerns.

> I actually don't think people know what widening participation is in this place … the debate in terms of widening participation has led to a number of new terms and phrases which fall into fair access, social mobility, access to professions and public benefit. (Staff 3 –widening participation manager HEI A)

This was mirrored by other members of staff who were interviewed at the three case study HEIs. Arguably there is a fundamental lack of interest and understanding in terms of social inclusion within HEIs.

> I'm being vague here but to be honest, I think this social inclusion and widening participation mean different things to different people. Widening participation is more like hands on getting people through the door whereas I think access means creating more of a community based side to widening participation. (Staff 24 – administration HEI C)

Interviewees within all three case study HEIs did raise concerns over the challenges of widening participation. Interviewees identified activities related to a wider societal level. The impact is based around the complexity, educational, social and cultural factors involved their interplay and their long term frames involved. The administrative staff at HEI B stated that recruitment, progression, achievement and retention are the fundamental aspects for individual groups. All three HEI staff interviewed recognised the strengths in providing transformative education, were ambitious in wishing to track impact beyond the HEIs wider society:

> The main impact we need to look at is to see if the policies and practices are being adhered to. We should see ourselves as here to have a positive impact on employability. The university's alumni are supporting and creating knowledge, affecting the economy, especially if there is data from the widening participation students. (Staff 4 – academic HEI B)

Staff interviewed emphasised the importance of appreciating that each student was very different and deserved respect and further to this walks a very different path, a fundamental social inclusion.

1   Stereotyping people because of their backgrounds does give
2   them a head start to being disadvantaged against. It is important
3   to understand that these individuals value their backgrounds and
4   part of their history. I actually grew up in a council estate and
5   came from a difficult background we need to appreciate that
6   people from BME or widening participation backgrounds can
7   bring a hell of a lot to the nation. We need to think about our
8   curricula where HEIs could really be acting as change agents
9   rather than HEIs reinforcing the view that already exists. (Staff
10   1 – academic HEI C)

11   The quote illustrates an informed leadership role for HEIs in
12 allowing for social inclusion and social mobility to become a reality.

13   I think I would be more excited about a project that raises
14   aspirations across the board not looking at FE but more at the
15   primary end where aspirations are driven up amongst under-
16   represented groups which are very much working class boys so
17   that you can get them to think about university at a very young
18   age and gaining a career anywhere in the world. (Staff 2 –
19   academic HEI C)

20   HEI B has renamed widening participation as Access and Widening
21 Participation. HEI B is attempting to direct social inclusion into a more
22 formal focus on widening participation.

23   In 2004 – widening participation at the university meant
24   something different to what it is considered as now. Now the
25   question 'how were we interpreting widening participation in
26   our practice? Well, I can tell you it didn't exist. It certainly wasn't
27   anything to do with social justice? (Staff 4 – academic HEI B)

28   This study has highlighted the importance of defining the success
29 of higher education in more individualised terms as an urgent priority
30 that the HEIs need to embrace if it is to appeal to the breadth of
31 diversity amongst prospective students.

32   Social inclusion of students from BME backgrounds is difficult
33   as we are not responsible for getting a certain group to attend
34   university. They should want to come and we need to address
35   the processes which they need to follow to apply for courses. …
36   I find it hard to understand why as HEIs we need to be seen to
37   be spending so much money on getting certain groups into
38   university rather than focusing our agenda for all. (Staff 29 –
39   administrator HEI B)

1   From findings there is view that social inequality is prevalent within
2   HEIs. Findings from staff illustrated that BME students don't behave
3   like their White middle class peers they are very much at a disadvantage
4   regardless of their educational attainment.

5   ## Recruitment and Retention

6   Staff viewpoints were gained from all three case study HEIs:

7   We have brilliant academic colleagues who come in on
8   weekends, summer holidays to work on outreach programmes
9   for free so there is some commitment to recruiting widening
10   participation students. So we do look into widening participation
11   and try and see if we can recruit the good BME students. ... But
12   it er ... can be difficult ... (Staff 13 – academic HEI C)

13   Staff member 13 interviewed at HEI C believed that commitment
14   towards widening participation was very varied. Institutionally,
15   academic and administrative staff did not feel that their role was to
16   recruit students and in particular work towards recruiting BME
17   students. The three case study HEIs illustrated from the findings that
18   institutional commitment towards recruitment and retention of BME
19   students was weakly framed. Staff who are committed to widening
20   participation and in particular, BME recruitment and retention find
21   themselves in a situation where they are unable to make any
22   contribution to widening participation as such commitment goes
23   against the institutional culture. At institutional level, the three case
24   study HEIs did have a considerable choice over the various
25   government measures for student recruitment and retention purposes.
26   The case study HEIs had a considerable amount of negotiation
27   between what they wanted to include from the national widening
28   participation government agenda.

29   We are concerned more about the figures and not really about
30   the benchmarks set out by the government as such ... by
31   including students from BME and the widening participation
32   backgrounds we could quite easily increase our student numbers.
33   (Staff 13 – academic HEI C)

34   The statement outlined above was very different from the ideology
35   set out by case study HEI A. Staff 13 – HEI A widening participation
36   manager did state that there were issues that surround the benchmark
37   guidelines initiated by HEFCE:

38   As a university, we are reasonably positioned. We are trying to

work with outside bodies to improve our intake of BME student numbers as well as work with widening participation programmes. (Staff 13 – academic HEI C)

The statement outlined indicates that the government's aspirations to gaining an increased number of students from under-represented groups but shows the limitations associated with the case study HEI approaches. There is very little evidence that the case study HEIs are actually moving forward to address concerns over BME recruitment and retention.

Our objectives are set against performance indicators and benchmarks which are initiated by HEFCE/HESA. This does then mean that subject qualifications take precedence over the type of student we are recruiting. (Staff 13 – academic HEI C)

HEFCE's agenda is not something that case study HEI A wanted to adopt. Fundamentally there was some difficulty in all three case study HEIs actually understanding the balance between the government's benchmark requirements.

I am going to come across negative but the structures within this institution don't support the government agenda. Our focus is to hold onto the gold standard students ... I mean students who have the A levels, who come from good school have middle class parents who will encourage their children. (Staff 19 – widening participation manager HEI B)

HEI C – widening participation manager:

Within this institution, we need to focus on driving up quality; we are looking for quality students, which does mean that the focus tends to be on students who come from good schools with top qualifications, which does go against the widening participation agenda. (Staff 6 –widening participation manager HEI C)

The three case study HEIs were consistent in trying to achieve government funding in their recruitment and retention processes.

It's interesting to see that with government policy in place which is very much trying to ensure that non-traditional students attend higher education doesn't seem to be working in reality... I've realised though once you have got these students, they do actually engage. (Staff 3 – widening participation manager HEI A)

1   The sentiments outlined by staff member 3 were reiterated by HEI
2 C academic:

3   The strategy is very much to maximise income where possible
4   and when we look at where the money will come from then it
5   puts things into perspective … so yes the aim is to have as many
6   BME or widening participation student attending our
7   institution. We have changed the way we work, which helps to
8   increase government funding … at the point which non-
9   traditional students register we get a considerable amount of
10   funding… (Staff 2 – academic HEI C)

11   BME recruitment and retention is clearly muddied within the
12 widening participation construct implemented by government policy.
13 Widening participation remains a conflicted discourse whereby
14 contradictory impulses around aspiration, university based support for
15 recruitment and retention are clearly not embedded within the strategic
16 approach to social inclusion. As the recruitment and retention of BME
17 students is embedded within the widening participation national policy
18 this is not underpinned at institutional level. Each member of staff
19 interviewed did specifically remark on the challenge of embedding
20 BME recruitment and retention without embedding it within widening
21 participation policy.

22   I think as staff we understand the necessity to recruit BME
23   students… however, I'm not too sure how diverse the groups
24   we get are… I do know that widening participation is a term we
25   use to ensure recruitment and retention but to what extent we
26   recruit and retain BME students is unclear to me anyway…
27   (Staff 20 – admissions administrator HEI B)

28   Limited diversity within staff was perceived to hinder recruitment
29 and retention:

30   I think if the staff at university were more of a diverse group that
31   would help, most of my lecturers are White, middle class which
32   doesn't really respond to diversity in recruitment and retention.
33   (Staff 28 – administrator HEI B)

34   Recruitment and retention was an issue for all three case study
35 HEIs. Limited diversity was a concern within all three case study HEIs.
36 Interviewees were concerned about the student centred measures of
37 impact on recruitment and retention of students from BME
38 backgrounds.

1 It might feel as though register taking is unimportant but actually
2 we want to show the students that we actually do care about
3 them and actually want them to come to university and study.
4 (Staff – 13 academic HEI C)

5 As part of the recruitment and retention process and to encourage
6 student admissions HEI A and B offered the opportunity for bursaries
7 for recruitment and retention purposes the Russell group HEI A
8 admission staff emphasised the need for high A level results regardless
9 of ethnicity.

10 We encourage applications from students who can achieve high
11 A level grades – we can't really include Access Agreement
12 recommendations at all stages… as we are not an institution
13 which compromises entry requirements for the sake of being
14 politically correct. (Staff 3 –widening participation manager HEI
15 A)

16 HEI A widening participation manager believed that the HEI was
17 justified in the decision to be academically selective:

18 We cannot compromise on academic standards but I understand
19 that the issue of recruiting BME students is an important one –
20 but I'm not sure how it's all going to be sorted out. (Staff 3 –
21 widening participation manager HEI A)

22 Interviewees were asked to measure the impact on institutional level
23 and the tensions that are evident between staff in terms of recruitment
24 and retention.

25 In terms of impact measurements data that the HEI has is far
26 from accurate. (Staff 23 – admin HEI B).

27 Interviewees were asked about measures in terms of BME student
28 centeredness when considering BME within the widening participation
29 actively and strategy. Although there was further concern over the
30 retention of BME students:

31 It's amazing how many BME students drop out after the first
32 few weeks of starting their courses – we have to report findings
33 back and there is a significant drop. (Staff 21 admin HEI A)

34 We have tried to keep track of BME students and monitor their
35 progress but it is difficult to appreciate as some academics don't
36 even complete registers. (Staff 23 – admin HEI B)

37 We have a good system in place we think but we can only act on

1 feedback we get from staff teaching BME students. (Staff 24 –
2 admin HEI C)

3 HEI B Staff 17 believed that widening participation is about
4 recruitment and promotion of the course. However, it was worrying to
5 see that staff at HEI B believed that recruitment and retention of
6 widening participation students were concerned with simply getting
7 them through the doors.

8 Widening participation is something that the institution does to
9 bring in non- traditional students. It is important to concentrate
10 more on the course design, progression, study and skills which
11 if put correctly into place would help into recruitment and
12 retention. (Staff 17 admin HEI B)

13 The notion that teaching non-traditional students were difficult to
14 deal with was clear from interview feedback provided by staff 2. There
15 was a strong belief that non- traditional students were not able to deal
16 with the demands of HEI study once they had arrived at the institution.

17 Widening participation needs to really look at widening access
18 to students. With the access agreement, the aim was to improve
19 learning environments which would allow individuals to access
20 courses but the problem is what do we do with them when they
21 get here? It's important to support students to achieve successful
22 outcomes. By student access the students entering the institution
23 by any means but we owe it to the BME students to become as
24 successful as they can – it's how those students succeed. (Staff 2
25 – academic HEI C).

26 There was a common understanding regarding the role of the
27 organisation; there was further confusion about what widening
28 participation was and what the institution was supposed to do about it.

29 There are some unfortunate points to understand in terms of
30 widening participation. HEIs considered as poor HEIs are
31 associated with branding. Problems as an institution we need to
32 think about aspiring these BME groups of students and we don't
33 seem to be doing that at the moment. (Staff 18 – academic HEI
34 A)

35 The staff did believe that BME students struggled with the
36 motivation and limited support mechanisms in place at HEI's. In all
37 three case study HEIs widening participation was in existence but
38 unfortunately at operational level staff were not aware of specific

documentation which they could use to address operational concerns of BME students. Findings are in line with the view that HEIs are creating policy documentation but are failing to adhere to it where necessary for students. Social class plays a fundamental role in the negative experiences felt by BME students at HEI level. This was reiterated through interviews with students. 15% of BME students interviewed felt so isolated that they were prepared to withdraw from their studies. The research findings highlight that regardless of a larger number of BME students actually attending HEIs at undergraduate level support mechanisms were not in place to provide an inclusive environment for these students. At HEI A staff 30 commented on how some of their colleagues were racially biased during the admissions process:

> Some of my colleagues not all are very selective as to who they think should be at university. They don't if I'm being honest… want to let the blacks and Pakistanis in. (Staff 30 HEI A)

There is an increase in racial bias when allocating HEI places, which supports the views of staff 30.

Learning, Teaching and Assessment

To understand a cross-institutional view of widening participation from a strategic context finding were examined in relation to each of the case study HEIs. Findings support the notion that HEI's A and B are chasing government policy funding drivers.

> I believe they are used interchangeably. I understand that they shouldn't be though… I think the institution has been caught up with the government policy drivers, the other positioning here is the philosophical positioning which looks at ensuring that those students who have not traditionally engaged within higher education, are able to and in doing so allow widening participation to retain students and allow them to achieve. (Staff 4 - academic HEI B)

This view was mirrored by HEI A academic staff.

> The view that widening participation is something we have to consider when students are here – studying, this is something we should look at earlier on though – we can improve widening participation through course design, progression, study and skills we do need to think about the support available to all students – there is some concern about assessments within HEI

A particularly when some colleagues choose to assess in a formal, structured manner. (Staff 15 –academic HEI A)

HEI C academic staff believed that it was the responsibility of colleagues to address BME student concerns and make every effort with their teaching, learning and assessment strategies to create inclusive learning.

Widening participation is taking students with intellectual ability which allows them then to benefit from higher education which really we try to encourage and support in particular with their teaching, learning and assessment. It's about the sociological aspects of people benefitting from going to university. (Staff 2- academic HEI C)

From findings, staff 2 and staff 1 were able to contextualise widening participation concepts and had some understanding as to the concerns of BME students within HEIs.

For our institution widening participation is about achievement, attainment, progression and retention. We aim to give these students the best possible learning experience which can be seen as comparable to any other student not from a widening participation background... I do understand that the whole idea of widening participation is to provide support to these students. I appreciate that this cannot always be achieved even within our institution. Colleagues have a different perspective and different understanding of widening participation. (Staff 1 – academic HEI C)

In contrast to this at institutional level, there are insufficient funds which do not support the retention of students from BME – widening participation backgrounds. The three case study HEIs do not embed widening participation within the curriculum. A curriculum focussing on the learning, teaching and assessment of students from BME backgrounds, in particular, is essentially absent where cultural values and beliefs are not addressed.

There are pockets of development regarding the curriculum, where curriculum, issues around retention and progression do get addressed but again this is ad- hoc. (Staff 1– academic HEI C)

The interviewees suggested that there were issues which hindered greater inclusivity in the curriculum.

In most HEIs… the strategy has been to maximise income and I think that's generally accepted. (Staff 3 - academic HEI A)

From the staff interviews throughout the three case study HEIs it was consistent that there was a commitment to inclusive teaching and assessment practices. However, there was a considerable omission in terms of the teaching, learning and assessment strategies that had specifically reduced the BME attainment gap. Although some staff believed that was taking place within the university the staff interviewed were unable to state where clearly this occurred. A strong belief across all three case study HEIs where staff were interviewed believed that some assessments privileged particular groups of students. There were some concerns raised from staff interviews where there was concern over the lower expectations set for BME students.

I'm not happy about finding ways to target single groups, all HEIs need to look at ways in which they can support BME groups from the perspectives of structurally, institutionally, strategically and become embedded within the institution. (Staff 14- academic HEI C)

Staff were signifying commitment towards widening participation; however, unclear about how to create and deliver inclusive learning programmes for BME students. The next section examines the operational level findings in terms of the student perspective.

Students were asked to describe their experiences within the school, FE and HE sector and to highlight specific incidences they felt were pertinent to their learning. Over 75% of all the BME students who were interviewed expressed negative school experiences, where teachers and Careers officers were not expecting them to pass their GCSE and A Levels and proceed to University, where they were encouraged to take up sports, placed in lower streams and non-exam classes as illustrated by the comment of this student:

When I told my Careers Officer that I wanted to go to University, he looked at me in complete and utter amazement, as if to say - are you sure you are all right? (Student 5 HEI A)

Students still talk with anger and bitter regret when they recalled their past school experiences:

My general experience in the education system ... (pauses and thinks for a while) ... you see the thing is that teachers and lecturers did not give me enough attention, they did not

1   understand my cultural and academic needs, I just was not taken
2   seriously. It's like I was there just to fill in the numbers, but my
3   history, my cultural background, my language, and my whole
4   being as a BME young person growing up in Britain was seen as
5   insignificant. I know its sounds odd to say this, but it is very
6   painful to be present in those situations and yet be invisible. It
7   is a very painful experience, considering the effort it takes for a
8   BME student to jump all the hurdles of schooling just to get to
9   University. (Student 15 HEI A)

10   **Figure 10.** Operational Level Thematic Analysis

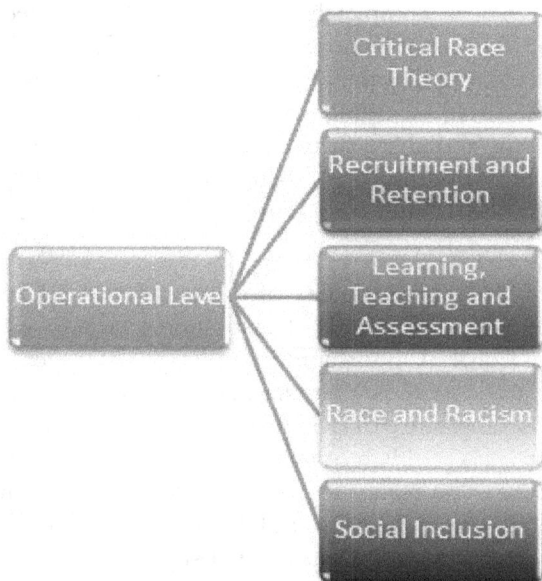

11

12   50 per cent of students found that even where the school
13 curriculum tried to address the experiences of BME people in Britain
14 and the world, the subject content was very shallow, that it was taught
15 from a Eurocentric perspective, and that the knowledge and
16 experiences of BME students in class or BME people with such
17 knowledge within the community were not utilised. As a result, most
18 students saw these lessons as marginal, not important, and not subject
19 to the same academic rigour as other subject areas. For example,
20 students within the three case study HEIs found it quite frustrating
21 with limited exploration of the exploitation of BME people and their
22 contribution to the British economy. This view was confirmed by
23 White academics identified a range of problems faced by BME students
24 in HEIs. These included negative experiences of the previous

1 schooling, particularly in terms of low teacher expectations and
2 difficulties in discovering themselves or their identities owing to
3 curricula being insufficiently inclusive of their cultural, social and
4 historical background. BME students were faced with racism both
5 from academic staff within HEI and within placement organisations.
6 Some students saw the problems they experienced as emanating from
7 the structural changes in the funding arrangements brought by the
8 HEFCE:

9 At the University there is very little time when tutors have one-
10 to-one relationship with students. In some cases the personal
11 tutorial system has been completely cut off. This has created
12 difficulties for BME students who would have benefited from
13 the support and guidance that the personal tutorial system used
14 to offer. This also would be a time when BME students would
15 voice their problems and share their experiences, and at times
16 would change the tutor's attitude and behaviour in the way they
17 viewed and treated BME students. That opportunity has been
18 lost. (Student 70 HEI C)

19 One of the major barriers to equality of opportunity in HEIs for
20 BME students is the pervasive nature of institutional racism. Whilst
21 most HEIs have Equal Opportunities policies, however the
22 experiences of BME students show that racism exists in its most subtle
23 forms. Sometimes the language of HEIs mission statements gives the
24 impression that there is no problem of racism, and therefore it is not a
25 serious topic of debate. The reality for BME students is that covert
26 racism is a common feature of their life, and that this makes it difficult
27 to tackle racism. As the comment of this student suggests:

28 The racism in this institution is very subtle. Sometimes the
29 racism I am talking about is not even apparent to some BME
30 students. It is certainly not always apparent to White students or
31 lecturers. At times when you mention that you have experienced
32 racism, White friends and lecturers turn round and look
33 surprised as if to say, how could you say such a thing, when we
34 have been with you most of the time and we have not seen you
35 experiencing racism. That's how subtle that racism is. As a result
36 to be honest some BME students don't bother to raise issues of
37 racism because it appears that you are just nit-picking and being
38 petty. (Student 44 HEI B)

39 Most BME students commented that the racism that they
40 experienced on a day-to-day basis was being marginalised not only by

White academics but by the liberal ethos in most HEIs that makes it difficult for both staff and students to discuss the issues of unequal treatment of BME students. One area of general misunderstanding was when White female staff tried to make connections between racism and other forms of oppression, and in particular sexism. Interviews with White staff showed that several had introduced the issue of gender, perhaps an inequality of which they had more direct understanding or experience. One male respondent found that issues of sexuality presented more difficulties than issues of racism. There was indication that White women staff attempted to use their understanding of gender and experience of sexism to try to understand and raise the issue of racism. BME students on the other hand whilst acknowledging the relevance of finding common threads in other forms of oppression, they felt that sometimes White feminists did this to minimise issues of racism under discussion:

> White female lecturers talk about solidarity between feminists and anti- racists, I am not quite sure whether they are serious about this or just playing a game. I do not want someone to come and empathise with my plight and yet they do not challenge the racist and sexist practices that pervade the institution. Why is it that I am the only BME woman on the course, and why is it that all the research students in this department are White? This is no coincidence you know, and where is the solidarity there? The way I look at it, solidarity has to be put in practice, we cannot say one thing and yet be seen to be doing nothing about some of the oppressive practices that BME students have to put up with in these HEIs. (Student 35 HEI B)

This view was reinforced by another female student in a different course. This leads us to believe that these views are not isolated incidents, but are common experiences of BME students in most courses.

> What I found at times very upsetting and frustrating was that whenever there was a heavy discussion about the experiences of BME students or BME people in general with White female lecturers, invariably that subject would be quickly switched to a related or distant issue on gender or sexism. I am a positive BME woman. I know that sexism pervades most of these HEIs. Issues of gender and sexism are very closely linked, but I strongly object to the way that debates or discussions on racism tend to

be high jacked and thus marginalised, and yet issues of racism are very important to all BME students. (Student 55 HEI B)

One of the constant themes mentioned by BME students and White staff is the need for HEIs to employ more BME staff. A statement made by one student summarises the feeling that the majority of the BME students felt.

HEIs from my experience are a facade of neutrality in dealing with the racial inequalities. Firstly, there are far too few BME academics on the teaching staff. White teachers learn about racism from text books, they don't live it, they hear and read about it. This is very frustrating as it leaves (once again) little room for the experiences of BME students to be brought into the debate. (Student 78 HEI C)

It is over the attitudes of White staff that BME students were most vociferous. This varied from not being taken seriously as students to having no BME expression within the curriculum. The theme of limited understanding and in some cases total lack of sensitivity of BME experience and reality ran through all the responses. Most BME students felt that White academics were playing a game with anti-racism, they were not convinced that most White academic staff fully understand the nature, extent and negative effects that racism had on BME students, as illustrated by the comments of student, 17, 38 and 31:

I cannot count how many times I have sat in lectures or seminars and heard White lecturers talking and lecturing about racism and yet they themselves are act in a racist manner and are unable to deal with or confront their own racism. (Student 17 HEI A)

Frankly I am sick and tired of being told that I should act like any other student in this institution by White staff who don't understand what I am going through. I am not asking for favours, but when I have a legitimate request for something that I feel is culturally relevant to me and I am entitled to, lecturers should not accuse me of wanting special treatment. I don't want special treatment, all I want is that my point of view is heard and that my request is acknowledged, that is all. (Student 38 HEI B)

They did not express their racist comments in my presence, and that was very hypocritical of them. But some White students told me of racists statements made about myself or other BME students in my absence. Some comments made by lecturers

1 suggested that my presence on the course was not particularly
2 welcomed. That's how it makes you feel. (Student 31 HEI B)

3   There were frequent references to racist attitudes and practices by
4 White lecturers, over 50% cited having racist lecturers and in four cases
5 there were verbal and physical confrontations with staff, and BME
6 students saw these confrontations not as isolated incidents but as
7 everyday occurrences as stated by student 40:

8   While lecturers think of racism as an academic subject, to them
9   it's another theoretical concept to be analysed and
10   deconstructed, there is nothing wrong with that. But the
11   difference here is that we live it and experience it every day, it is
12   not just a theoretical concept that appears in and reappears in
13   lectures and seminars. We live it daily. When sometime we
14   remind those lecturers that what they have just said or done is
15   racist by definition if not by intent, they become very sensitive.
16   They forget that they cannot be immune from the history of
17   imperialism, colonialism, slavery, etc. That needs to be
18   acknowledged, otherwise they will never realise the amount of
19   racism that has been passed on to them by accident of history.
20   (Student 40 HEI B).

21   Staff at all three case study HEIs did raise concerns regarding racism
22 which existed institutionally and that racism was very much militated
23 against the BME student. Racism was deemed a societal problem and
24 not one where the HEI could address any concerns regarding
25 institutional racism:

26   We don't have an individual member of staff who is racist......I
27   am not saying that but every university works within a set
28   structure. My example is very much around how the assessments
29   are very much tailored towards White middle class students.
30   These assessments and structures are not conducive to BME
31   students. (Staff 9 HEI A)

32   Additional to this HEI structures were considered to be a limitation
33 to progress for BME students. There were inadequate complaint
34 mechanisms, poor pedagogic practices. The two semester structure is
35 based on a Christian calendar which did not meet the religious diversity
36 of the diverse student body. Staff related the attainment gap amongst
37 BME students to the students themselves. Staff felt that BME students
38 had insufficient knowledge and inadequate language skills to deal with
39 HEI learning, teaching and assessment. Staff interviewed within all

three case study HEIs felt that the structures and practices of HEIs favoured White middle class students and discriminated against BME students. There was a strong concern throughout all three case study HEIs that there should be a commitment to inclusive learning, teaching and assessment practices. However, when staff interviewed it was transparent that there was no clear learning strategy to address BME attainment. High expectations were not put forward for BME students.

> I am hesitant to put forward or single out BME students or any other student for that matter. I don't think that it is a fair method to support students. (Staff 4 HEI B)

Support for students should be multifaceted so that students can access support as required:

> Some support is appropriate for some students and some support is appropriate for other students. There needs to be some form of differentiation. (Staff 13 HEI C)

Staff and students drew on the lack of integration mechanisms within the HEIs to support BME students.

Social Inclusion

Regardless as to how many students are integrated into the UK educational system they are inevitably met with barriers to educational inclusion. Feedback from BME students illustrated some points consistent with negative impact from their families. The concerns are outlined by student 5:

> We have limitations and are responsible for our household as we as having to study. Whereas the White students can go clubbing and partying and don't come across as having other family commitments....I have to take other things into consideration and basically I am judged by the community that I live in. It is hard. This is who I am and I have to show my family that I am a good son. My family have expectations which I have to meet and I can't push these expectations to one side. (student 66 HEI C)

BME students had a strong view that as BME students their ethnicity played a considerable role in the way they were taught and their academic results. Additionally BME students felt that they had considerable pressures from their home life that fundamentally added to the negative output for their studies. 86% of BME students interviewed believed that parental lack of knowledge of higher education played a considerable part in misunderstandings in terms of higher education expectations where family life would take precedence. Socio-demographic factors concerning widening participation BME students were derived as negative contributors towards the social inclusion of these students. BME students felt that their poor initial schooling environments did not help them at university level:

> The other students went into the labs and looked at the equipment and instantly knew what to do...I felt a bit isolated as I had never seen half of the stuff there. I think a lot of the students in the room had been to private school....I guess. I felt a little awkward and didn't want to touch anything just in case I looked stupid. (Student 12 HEI A)

Social divide which exists in education for BME students and that of widening participation is far more widespread than what the government wishes to acknowledge. Students from BME groups felt lack of support from staff in improving their confidence, helping BME students to adapt to the social and academic constraints of university life.

> I was thrown out of my tutorial.... I thought I could go to the toilet walk in and out of the tutorial room if I wanted to.... I didn't think I needed to get permission. I went to answer a call and this tutor picked up my bag and put it outside of the room.... I was pretty upset about that.... I did make a complaint but nothing was ever done about it. I didn't get an apology or anything like that. (Student 77 HEI C)

BME students felt that their HEIs have failed them in terms of academically but also to create social inclusion. Staff failed to integrate BME students into the wider group setting. As a result BME students felt alienated and in particular where they had to interact in group work assessments. BME students interviewed in all three case study HEIs felt secluded and overlooked by White middle class students. Findings illustrated that during lectures White middle class students would sit separately from the BME group of students. Tutorial and seminar settings were where BME students felt that again White middle class students would group together and avoid any real contact with BME students.

> There is no cultural belonging in this place. My example is me...why doesn't it show on my records that I used to be homeless and had no support from anywhere. My tutors should

be monitoring me and asking me for meetings to make sure I feel OK about everything. My only support really is from friends of mine. That nurturing environment doesn't exist at this university and that nobody was interested in me in my first few weeks here really is an important statement. (Student 8 HEI A)

BME students did emphasise that there was very limited inter-ethnic integration. However this was not something that staff at all three HEIs raised as concerns. For students this was a considerable issue, students argued that HEI staff teaching them should do more to support BME students so that they could feel a sense of belonging within the group rather than having a feeling of isolation and being ignored. BME students in particular Asian students did not embrace the nightlife and drinking alcohol:

My White peers like to go on bar crawls when we have guest lectures or tutorials we tend to have a selection of alcoholic drinks, as I don't drink alcohol I feel it is harder to mix and feel accepted. So I tend to stand out from my peers and automatically feel isolated. (Student 21 HEI A)

Marketing material was considered to be misleading and presenting an unrealistic and deceitful image of university life.

The university website shows a black student with a White girl and other colours and you think wow – but when you actually start studying it becomes pretty clear that there is no mix like that. You are given the impression that students mix and get on with each other from different backgrounds but in reality they don't. (Student 32 HEI B)

Widening participation for BME students showed considerable inadequacies present within the learning, teaching and assessment strategies. Within HEI B staff did not support BME student concerns. Staff interviews from HEI B illustrated that there were fundamental societal and structural barriers which encompassed poverty, political support for widening participation in context of BME students and the fundamental concerns of decreasing the educational construct for BME students. Family pressures meant that BME students were restricted from engaging fully within student life and studying to higher degrees. Cultural differences had a tremendous impact on BME students' feeling a sense of belonging within their HEI. BME student responses meant that their feelings and need to feel that they belonged within the institution was an important factor for them, responses illustrated that there were large scale discrepancies as to the responsibility of social inclusion for BME students. There were concerns by BME students who felt that there were discrepancies between the White middle class students and that of the students coming from BME backgrounds. Staff responses were interesting as requests from staff were requesting greater institutional structures in place that would allow for allow for BME issues and widening participation to be addressed. In all three case study HEIs widening participation for BME students documentation existed but this was not passed down to staff. The learning, teaching and assessment practices did not address BME student needs and therefore were deemed inconsequential. Additionally student family and cultural background played a considerable role in the measures to create social inclusion. Social inclusion inadequacies were a fundamental throughout the findings for this study. BME students felt that staff had failed them not only through the academic side but also failed to integrate them within the wider group of students, leaving them feeling alienated. Additionally, findings suggested BME students have to struggle to feel accepted within HEIs, and little is done to formulate social inclusion.

Recruitment and Retention

Within the three case study HEIs significance has been attached to the in-reach and out-reach programmes. Within the case study HEIs the bulk of the widening participation work was based around the pre-entry stages of recruitment. 64% of support was provided for pre-entry recruitment of widening participation students. 6% of widening participation support was allocated towards the retention of widening participation students. Open days inviting widening participation students were considered as an important element of the three case study HEI initiatives. HEI A replaced taster days with challenge days, this is where widening participation students were given the opportunity to experience the courses which the students had applied for. HEI B tailored open days to subject specific days. In contrast it was interesting to observe that HEI C did not address recruitment initiatives as ardently as HEI A and B.

Recruitment was on an ad-hoc basis with limited initiatives to support widening participation and BME initiatives. Special access schemes within the three case study HEIs were limited in support of students from under-represented groups. Offering a range of courses for example the foundation degrees, part-time learning opportunities did show some aspects of ensuring recruitment from widening

1 participation backgrounds but the routes outlined by the HEIs did not
2 address BME recruitment and retention opportunities. HEI A offered
3 foundation degrees, however there was no evidence that the
4 foundation degrees supported BME entrants. The foundation degrees
5 were seen as tailored towards the lower ability students and it is
6 fundamental to state here that BME students are not all of lower ability
7 therefore BME students would not be interested in programmes for
8 which they are over qualified for. Staff interviewed at all three case
9 study HEIs stated that retention was a concern for them.

10   It might be a bit childlike but we need to take registers in a more
11   professional manner and not an ad-hoc basis. I think that
12   colleagues need to take ownership of taking registers and see this
13   as a positive rather than a negative. We need to monitor
14   attendance and see it as a positive to monitor BME attendance.
15   (Staff 19 – HEI B)

16   HEI A and B targeted recruitment and retention through tailoring
17 their programmes to widening participation initiatives. The emphasis
18 was largely around the pre-entry and admission stages (Francis, 2006).
19 Recruitment and retention within all three case study HEIs seemed to
20 be based around pre-entry and admissions. The widening participation
21 manager argued that there was a clear boundary with his role:

22   My role stops when they get through the door. I don't deal with
23   the support side when they get here. Tutors tend to deal with
24   that sort of thing. But I'm sure that side of things is covered
25   properly by our staff. (Staff 3 – HEI A)

26   It was worrying that over the three case study HEIs there was no
27 real on-going support for BME students and administrative and
28 academic staff felt that they were not responsible for the retention of
29 BME students and that this was a senior management responsibility.
30 There is a lack of transparency where HEIs are recruiting students, as
31 outlined in findings from all three case study HEIs. HEIs are more
32 concerned with gaining competitively rather than including under-
33 represented groups. All three case study HEIs did pick and choose
34 elements of the widening participation strategy and what the HEI felt
35 was more in line with their strategic position. HEIs were fully aware of
36 the stereotypes which are attached to HEIs that are socially inclusive
37 environments. HEI A and B were mostly concerned with recruiting
38 students from middle class backgrounds. 62% of BME students argued
39 that admissions staff were unsupportive and lacked an understanding
40 of cultural complexities when BME students approached them for

support.

Learning, Teaching and Assessment

BME students, were asked whether or not they found widening participation useful for their studies at university responses were negative. The respondents did not feel this support existed. Personal tutors were deemed unhelpful and unsupportive. Student views were they felt that if the students could not cope with the pressures of university life then they should leave or withdraw.

> We don't get the same marks as the White students. I've never
> seen a BME student get a first - I really can't tell you why but I
> always get a border mark of 67 to 68. I'm not saying that this is
> because our names are different and then we don't get the marks
> but maybe I'm not clever enough or maybe we misunderstand
> what the lecturer tells us? Maybe their work is better than ours.
> I don't know but sometimes I think they get different feedback
> than we do. They e-mail their tutors and get more out of them
> than we do – so maybe we should be a bit more proactive.
> (Student 3 HEI A)

When Asian students try to fit into the UK educational system they are met with negative attitudes. Students felt that when they were knowingly downgraded in modules by staff they felt this was consistent with their ethnicity. Additionally BME students believed their under-attainment was related to limited and inconsistent support and feedback from staff was deemed unsupportive. Students felt that the work set was difficult to understand with no clarification from staff.

> I would say that we don't seem to achieve the same grade levels
> as the White students. I've never seen a black or Asian student
> on my course getting a 2:1s... I always get a 67 or 68 mark and
> my feedback is never clear as to why I got the mark I did....um
> maybe I think... we are not that clever, I sometimes think that
> the White students work is better than ours maybe? Some of my
> White friends email their tutors more than I do maybe I should
> be more active. (Student 49 HEI B)

Further to this the notion that BME students and in particular students from Asian backgrounds were rooted deeply in their cultural environment where it had become increasingly difficult for BME students to detach themselves from their culture in terms of their higher educational experience. Positive feedback from students did illustrate some support from students:

1   You get a quick response when you email tutors on my course.
2   My lecturers are pretty quick to respond to problems or
3   questions I have. I really like my tutors they care about me or at
4   least they show that they care about me. (Student 68 HEI C).

5   BME students were constructive in outlining that learning, teaching
6   and assessment practices were inadequate in terms of support and
7   guidance from staff, therefore reflecting negatively in terms of their
8   learning, teaching and assessment of their course. BME students were
9   asked about the support they received in terms of their assessments in
10   terms of their White peers, clear class barriers and racial barriers were
11   outlined here whereby BME students felt that their White peers
12   received more guidance and support continuously on their course.
13   Feedback from BME student interviews outlined distinct class barriers
14   evident in higher education. BME students were asked questions in
15   terms of their teaching, learning and assessments, 78% of BME
16   students interviewed felt they were not fully informed about
17   assessment requirements. All three case study HEIs where BME
18   students were interviewed felt that the assessments were written in an
19   academic style which BME students found difficult to relate to and
20   understand. BME students felt that they were not performing to a high
21   standard because they lacked clear and detailed feedback. Findings
22   suggest that BME students were extremely critical in terms of the
23   support they received from their tutors. There are distinctions between
24   how HEI staff behave and operate towards middle class White students
25   and BME students. BME students interviewed within the case study
26   HEIs felt that they were not provided with the time and support they
27   required in terms of their assessments.

28   University lecturers are given time and this university and in fact
29   bugger it – a lot of HEIs have not been proactive with us black
30   students. I have friends at other HEIs who say the same they
31   don't get the support and guidance in their assessments either
32   like me I mean…. I ask so many questions but the tutor looks at
33   me as if I am thick or something…from experience if you
34   approach a lecturer they always say to me go and fill out an
35   extension form or go and ask the counselling people. All I ask
36   for his to be seen as an individual and not a black man in a White
37   environment…cos this is sometimes I feel…..(Student 11 HEI
38   A)

39   5% of BME students did provide positive feedback when asked
40   about the level of teaching, learning and assessment support they had

1 been provided. What was exceptionally interesting was that the vast
2 majority – 95% of BME students interviewed believed that staff
3 teaching them were far from helpful, were abrupt and rude in many
4 cases. Therefore these students felt that they had to support each other
5 in terms of their teaching, learning and assessment.

6 I have a good network of friends, and we tend to support each
7 other. We try and motivate, guide and support each other,
8 because we want to try and get a good grade and we don't really
9 get anything back from the staff or our White peers. (Student 3
10 HEI A).

11 It was interesting to learn that BME students did not want targeted
12 support and this was consistent throughout all three case study HEIs.
13 BME students believed that targeted support would undermine them
14 in front of their peers, BME students felt that this would play into the
15 stereotypes of racism, this was something that would be considered
16 playing into the hands of the racists. If White middle class or White
17 working class students were not included in targeted support. BME
18 students did highlight that they would prefer to have structures in place
19 pinpointing peer assessment, academic skills provision and specific
20 teaching, learning and assessment support mechanisms through role
21 models which would support their learning, teaching and assessment
22 strategies. BME students felt that this was the most effective method
23 HEIs could implement.

24 When you start to look at people in terms of their skin colour
25 and profile people then start to think about role models and how
26 they fit into certain categories. There are then the perceptions
27 that BME people are doing quite badly. Why is it that we have
28 to be associated with black role models nobody ever mentions
29 White role models… sometimes I think things are made more
30 complicated than they need to be. (Student 8 HEI A).

31 Social inclusion concerns were evident through staff and student
32 interviews. Students felt that they lacked the pre-requisites for learning,
33 teaching and assessment within the institution, fundamental to this was
34 the inadequate level of support or guidance provided to the students to
35 which led to BME students failure in their module assessments. From
36 interview results students did hold the HEI and the staff responsible
37 for the issues they had which did not encourage their belonging within
38 the university environment. Student feedback from interview results at
39 all three HEIs illustrated that BME students felt that they were
40 regarded as second class citizens. BME students thought that they were

1   not supported academically and personally at their HEI. 15% of those
2   BME students were considering withdrawing from their studies as they
3   felt so isolated. Students and staff believed that measures needed to be
4   addressed to remove or reduce the attainment gap. There was a
5   necessity to consider that a greater commitment to inter-ethnic
6   integration was essential. Diversification and support mechanisms were
7   required to address social inclusion for BME students. Pastoral and
8   academic support was required for BME students and BME students
9   should be made aware of these mechanisms. Findings showed that
10   there was an uneven balance of BME students attending post 92 HEIs.
11   The level of BME students attending HEI A which were Russell Group
12   was much lower than those attending HEIs B and C. BME students
13   were accumulated in HEIs B and C. Racial bias was a concern for all
14   three case study HEIs particularly witnessed within the admissions
15   process. This is fundamental to BME representation within HEI A, B
16   and C. Staff as well as students in all three case study HEIs believed
17   racial bias existed within the admission process. HEI B interview
18   feedback illustrates racial bias:

19   My colleagues are somewhat selective when it comes to entry
20   into the institution. They want to keep the blacks or how shall I
21   say the erm....BME out wherever possible. The BMEs are a
22   difficult lot, some of them have been brought up here and still
23   can't string a sentence together in English so how will they be
24   able to complete a degree course... (laughs). (Staff 10
25   administrator HEI B)

26   HEI C staff interviewed believed that many of the BME students
27   wanted to avoid early marriage so decided to enrol onto a degree
28   course:

29   The BME students particularly those from Asian backgrounds
30   like the Pakistanis enrol onto courses so that they don't have to
31   marry which is a big concern for us. (Staff 24 administrator HEI
32   C)

33   BME students had lower attainment before they entered HEIs
34   when compared to their White middle class peers. BME students were
35   in the main non-traditional students, although Chinese and Indian
36   BMEs did take the traditional route into higher education. Pakistani
37   and Bangladeshi BMEs tended to achieve much lower grades than
38   those from Chinese and Indian backgrounds although when comparing
39   to black Caribbean students they tended to achieve much better grades.
40   Black Caribbean groups were much older and chose higher education

as a means of creating a better life for their families:

> I want to get a better job and this means so much to me for my
> children. I find that when I apply for anything I never get past
> the phone interview I feel so stupid. I challenged one company
> and they said that they had lots of people applying and that's
> why I didn't get it. (Student 24 HEI A)

Socio-economic status and lack of family support mechanisms played a fundamental role in attainment. Social inequality is prevalent within the case study HEIs. For recruitment and retention purposes BME students believed that if structure and social inclusion measures were correctly distributed within the HEIs then BME retention rates would increase. The findings highlighted the difficult and somewhat multiplicity of concerns associated with BME degree attainment, additional to this is the inter- sectional concern between ethnicity:

> I am conscious of a gap between BME students and that of
> White students.....additional to this I think the backgrounds of
> these students is considerably playing a part in this gap.....it
> seems like some of the BME students are going to university for
> the first time, additionally they have family pressures.....this
> causes significant differences between the White students and
> BME students. There are considerable social pressures faced by
> BME students when trying to achieve academically. (Staff 9 HEI
> A).

There was some concern from the findings that regardless of the types of questions put to staff there was a persistent reference to BME students having inadequate English skills and being unprepared to learn. BME students were seen as unprepared to study at HEI level. Across all three case study HEIs there was some evidence suggesting that there was a need for equality and diversity of the student body and a requirement to create a sense of belonging, particularly with the students from a variety of cultural backgrounds and therefore a need to create a strong cross cultural interaction. Regardless of this there was a lack of tailored inclusivity and therefore little evidence of BME specific inclusion models. Staff were unaware of the number of BME students attending their sessions, or courses:

> I'm not quite sure of the number of students attending my
> module who are BME students – I would need to check that...
> I think it might be in the line of 2% but they never turn up any
> way so you tend to ignore really......(Staff 2 HEI C)

1   The interview results signified above illustrate how staff at the three
2   case study HEIs were considerably alienated from BME students. Staff
3   knew that there was an attainment gap across the HEIs which still failed
4   to have any real understanding of how BME student faired with
5   teaching, learning and assessment.

6   I will need to check the surveys completed......its quite
7   embarrassing but I don't really know the answer to the
8   questions...(Staff 4 HEI B)

9   Staff felt that there was no gap between White and BME students
10   or were completely unaware of it:

11   Nothing has really bubbled up in that respect.......we have so
12   many different cultures here I don't think there is an issue. (Staff
13   13 HEI C)

14   Fundamentally staff discussed the unwillingness of colleagues to
15   address concerns around BME students, some staff it was felt were
16   reluctant to speak as they were more concerned about political
17   correctness or were scared they might say the wrong thing, which
18   meant that the issues of BME under-attainment were being ignored.
19   Further to this there was no formal method being used to address BME
20   under achievement. There were staff who were aware of an issue
21   surrounding BME attainment:

22   I am interested in knowing why there is such a big difference
23   between attainment and ethnicity......however I don't have
24   adequate support mechanisms within this institution to address
25   this concern. (Staff 19 HEI B)

26   However, this was a limited response as other staff member
27   questioned regarding BME attainment did not believe there was any
28   concern:

29   There's not much consideration or discussion of BME students
30   within our school.....it's not really an issue as otherwise we
31   would at least mention it......We have systems in place which
32   deal fairly and equally with all students...we as an institution do
33   not believe in positive discrimination. (Staff 3 HEI A)

34   There was a consensus that senior management did not have a clear
35   idea of a gap between attainment between BME and White students
36   but at a more local level staff were aware that BME students were
37   struggling and that there was a gap between attainment. Staff within
38   HEI C did concede that some students did achieve better than others,

1 in particular concerning retention and success which was related to
2 societal inequalities, relating to limited social, economic or cultural
3 aspects:

4   Certain groups will always under-perform and have
5   disadvantages......we can't really do anything about it at this
6   level....(Staff 18 HEI A)

7   This point was significant as staff 18 showed that there was an
8 understanding that there was an attainment gap but the HEI was not
9 prepared to address this. 70% of BME students interviewed argued that
10 they were given lower grades than their White counterparts and limited
11 feedback. When BME students were placed in groups the BME
12 students felt that they were already penalised. 83% of BME students
13 were dissatisfied with the feedback provided to them by staff. In taught
14 sessions BME students again felt that they were ignored or not
15 supported by staff, this was a fundamental concern. BME students at
16 all three case study HEIs stated that the White students did not want
17 to work with them when it came to group work. They felt that as BMEs
18 they were deemed lazy, and stupid. 62% of BME students felt that they
19 were isolated from educational life and ignored by staff when
20 requesting support. BME students believed that they were not
21 informed about assessments correctly and therefore they
22 misinterpreted the assessment requirements resulting in them failing
23 their assessments, again findings suggested, that, there is a clear
24 distinction between how staff behave and support middle class White
25 students in comparison to BME students. This point was raised in
26 interviews where BME students stated that staff teaching them did not
27 or would not provide them with time and support when they requested
28 it.

29   Thirty staff were interviewed, ten staff from each case study HEI.
30 At each of the case study HEIs staff interviewed were unclear of
31 policies and practices when dealing with BME students and in
32 particular the HEI widening participation policy at HEI level. Almost
33 all staff interviewed believed that BME and widening participation
34 students should be treated holistically. Interviews with the admissions
35 teams and administrators illustrated a lack of clear understanding
36 regarding policies and practices throughout the HEI. Admissions staff
37 could not categorise BME students correctly. It was interesting to find
38 that 78% of staff interviewed believed that students with Anglo-Saxon
39 names were treated differently from students with BME names. BME
40 students with had low attainment in comparison to their White middle

1   class counterparts. During interviews it was evident that black
2   Caribbean students were older than other BME students. All three case
3   study HEIs had a bolt on approach to widening participation. A bolt
4   on approach suggests that there was little dedication at the HEIs for
5   widening participation. Regardless of staff at all three case study HEIs
6   arguing that they are committed to addressing concerns of under-
7   representation within the HEIs. The semi- structured interviews
8   allowed further exploration and analysis of the values informed
9   through their understanding of inclusive learning. The political nature
10   of widening participation and social inclusion has meant that widening
11   participation illustrates a critical stance on under-representation within
12   the three case study HEIs. The widening participation and social
13   inclusion at institutional level illustrated an out-dated, dangerous and
14   self-defeating deficit model. BME students are surrounded with
15   barriers to social inclusion. BME students felt isolated, and victimised
16   throughout their learning experience within all three case study HEIs.
17   The interviews signified the lack of formal support mechanisms for
18   BME students to utilise when they needed it. BME students felt that
19   under-attainment for them was associated with their cultural
20   background. 86% of BME students interviewed felt that their parents
21   were unfamiliar with higher education and therefore were not able to
22   have a study environment at home.

23

CHAPTER 9

DISCUSSION AND THEORISING THE FINDINGS

The purpose of this chapter is to investigate and critically appraise the findings and to create links with the literature as discussed in chapter two. In meeting the research objectives outlined in chapter one, the researcher has used a qualitative methodological approach. Firstly the five themes are addressed, secondly within this chapter and analysis of findings across all themes were examined before summarising the analytical discussion.

Figure 11. Thematic Analysis

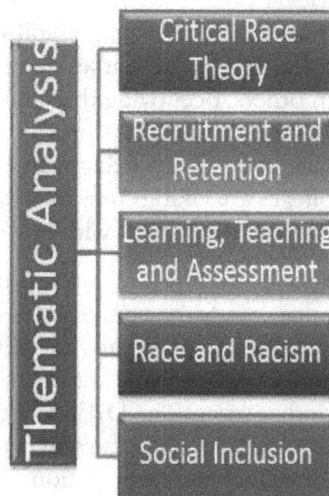

Extensive document analysis places importance on social inclusion, however, documentation regarding HEIs does not address fundamental concerns regarding race and racism, learning, teaching and assessment, recruitment and retention, social inclusion or the critical race theory construct. Document analysis at national level revealed significant limitations regarding national policy in terms of BME students. The national scholarship programme is part of the government's policy to get more young people from disadvantaged backgrounds into higher education – in particular into the country's most selective HEIs. The Access Agreement is based on supporting White working class boys and does not address concerns of limited inclusion of BME students. OFFA does stipulate that the organisation is there to promote fair access through the Access Agreement does not stipulate how BME students' needs and requirements are addressed. The Autumn Statement 2010 delivered by the coalition government aimed to provide 30,000 more student places for 2014-2015 in order to increase student numbers to 60,000 does not address BME inclusion. The Coalition Agreement 2010 aimed to increase access to the UK's top HEIs for students from low income backgrounds again does not stipulate any recommendations for BME students, furthermore, BME student access, recruitment, retention are not considered. The 2011 Consultation – "Higher Education Students at the Heart of the System" was aimed at delivering better student experience and taking more responsibility for increasing social mobility, the limited reference to BME students signifies the weaknesses within the widening participation national level policy. Women and ethnic minorities are well represented but participation levels are still low and those from poorer social classes. Poorer social classes have significantly lower participation rates than others, occupying the same low share of places on courses in 1999-00 as they did six years previously. The Department for Education and Skills, the Higher Education Funding Council for England, HEIs and colleges are taking steps to remove the obstacles to participation by people from the groups with low representation.

These obstacles include early loss of interest in education; poorer educational opportunities before applying to higher education; concerns about the benefits of taking part; and difficulties in securing financial support. There is scope to widen participation further by developing existing good practice. The DfES and the Funding Council have allocated over £200 million in the current academic year to HEIs and students to support widening participation. Whether these funds are targeted appropriately is a matter of concern: systematic information on the costs of HEIs' widening participation activities is not currently available, and the system of discretionary funding for poorer students is over complex and creates uncertainty for those students. The Department and the Funding Council have work in progress to address some of these problems. There is widespread activity by HEIs to raise aspirations in groups with low representation but much less to ensure that their applications have a fair chance of succeeding. Applicants from poorer social classes are less likely than others to succeed in converting their applications to accepted offers. Some HEIs have low participation by these groups because they do not attract many applications from them, while the problem for other HEIs is the high failure rate of applications from these groups. There is widespread concern that the current funding of higher education students and HEIs does not encourage a widening in participation by those from non- traditional backgrounds. While there are many factors that limit participation in higher education and more evidence is needed on the role finance plays, analysis of the case study HEI policy documentation suggest that the spectre of debt continues to influence many students and affects their risk/reward perceptions. The whole higher education sector is under-funded, but the financial position of certain HEIs that have a focus on widening participation is particularly serious. Benefiting little from the increase in research funding, but with higher costs in attracting and supporting non-traditional students, they are required to retrench. This could limit easy access to certain courses by those from non-traditional backgrounds. The sector is becoming increasingly polarised between the haves and the have-nots and the policies of the Government have failed to redress this sufficiently and may have inadvertently compounded the problem. Limited measures have been put in place to help the BME community. Government failure has forced course closures, threatened institutional shut downs, slashed Education Maintenance Allowance for FE college students by 60 per cent, and imposed draconian increases in tuition fees up to £9,000 a year on HE university students. The new student number allocation policy risks reversing gains in widening participation and social mobility. Students from less advantaged backgrounds are much less likely to achieve AAB grades and more likely to apply with Access qualifications, which cannot be included in the AAB+ population. The students most likely to gain from a degree do not just come in an 'AAB' package. HEIs will now also need to ensure that the HEFCE's 20% margin to recruit students from widening participation backgrounds is indeed used for this purpose. HEIs should also consider how they can strengthen their current efforts to prioritise AAB+ applicants from less advantaged backgrounds.

The 'economics of diversity' method is conceptually problematic for the enactment of a social justice approach. In other words, it treats social identities (such as those relating to social class, gender and ethnicity) as essential, static and clearly bounded phenomena, rather than recognising them as complex, shifting and contested interlinking indices. Despite an increasingly 'diverse' student population, higher

1 education's dominant academic culture continues to privilege, White,
2 middle-class and male values and practices, constructing the normative
3 student as an archetypal young, male, White, middle-class, independent
4 learner. Hence, policy analysis indicates that working-class, female,
5 mature and/or minority ethnic students, in particular, report feeling
6 alienated and ignored within the dominant academic culture even when
7 located in HEIs with 'diverse' student populations. Many working class
8 respondents feel that whilst they might be able to access higher
9 education, they feel little sense of entitlement or belonging there. In
10 this respect, the continued policy focus upon diverse student bodies as
11 dislocated from the structures and cultures of higher education is
12 missing/hiding a key area of concern for social justice.

13 ## Race and Racism/ Critical Race Theory

14 Discrimination of any kind and in particular racial discrimination in
15 education is considered as unlawful under the Race Relations
16 Amendment Act (2000). As discussed in previous chapters and
17 outlined in the Race Relations Amendment Act (2000) it is unlawful to
18 segregate an individual on racially motivated grounds. It is stipulated in
19 the Race Relations Act (2000) that racial discrimination should be non-
20 existent for any student wishing to participate in HEI study. The Race
21 Relations Act (2000) was amended to ensure that race equality duty is
22 fundamental to the Race Relations Act (2000) whereby it is significantly
23 outlined that the race equality duty for all HEIs should exist in
24 promoting race equality throughout all HEIs. The Race Relations
25 Amendment Act (2000) aims to promote the specific duties for HEIs
26 to prepare and maintain a race equality policy. All UK HEIs are
27 required to assess the impact of their policies in relation to different
28 racial groups. The Race Relations Amendment Act (2000) stipulates
29 that HEIs should evaluate the impact of the HEIs race equality policy
30 on students from different racial groups. The Race Relations
31 Amendment Act (2000) stipulates that HEIs should ensure that
32 assessment and monitoring is addressed through the HEI's racial
33 policy.

34

35

1   **Table 1.** Findings from results on Social Exclusion

Theme Race and Racism		
HEI A		
Student results	**Code**	**Comments**
Student	005	When I told my Careers Officer that I wanted to go to University, he looked at me in complete and utter amazement, as if to say - are you sure you are all right? (Student 5 HEI A)
Student	015	My general experience in the education system .... (pauses and thinks for a while) you see the thing is that teachers and lecturers did not give me enough attention, they did not understand my cultural and academic needs, I just was not taken seriously. It's like I was there just to fill in the numbers, but my history, my cultural background, my language, and my whole being as a BME young person growing up in Britain was seen as insignificant. I know its sounds odd to say this, but it is very painful to be present in those situations and yet be invisible. It is a very painful experience, considering the effort it takes for a BME student to jump all the hurdles of schooling just to get to University. (Student 15 HEI A)
Student	017	I cannot count how many times I have sat in lectures or seminars and heard White lecturers talking and lecturing about racism and yet they themselves are act in a racist manner and are unable to deal with or confront their own racism. (Student 17 HEI A)
HEI B		
Student results	**Code**	
Student	031	They did not express their racist comments in my presence, and that was very hypocritical of them. But some White students told me of racists statements made about myself or other BME students in my absence. Some comments made by lecturers suggested that my presence on the course was not particularly welcomed. That's how it makes you feel. (Student 31 HEI B)

Student	035	White female lecturers talk about solidarity between feminists and anti- racists, I am not quite sure whether they are serious about this or just playing a game. I do not want someone to come and empathise with my plight and yet they do not challenge the racist and sexist practices that pervade the institution. Why is it that I am the only BME woman on the course, and why is it that all the research students in this department are White? This is no coincidence you know, and where is the solidarity there? The way I look at it, solidarity has to be put in practice, we cannot say one thing and yet be seen to be doing nothing about some of the oppressive practices that BME students have to put up with in these HEIs. (Student 35 HEI B)
Student	038	Frankly I am sick and tired of being told that I should act like any other student in this institution by White staff who don't understand what I am going through. I am not asking for favours, but when I have a legitimate request for something that I feel is culturally relevant to me and I am entitled to, lecturers should not accuse me of wanting special treatment. I don't want special treatment, all I want is that my point of view is heard and that my request is acknowledged, that is all. (Student 38 HEI B)
Student	040	While lecturers think of racism as an academic subject, to them it's another theoretical concept to be analysed and deconstructed, there is nothing wrong with that. But the difference here is that we live it and experience it every day, it is not just a theoretical concept that appears in and reappears in lectures and seminars. We live it daily. When sometime we remind those lecturers that what they have just said or done is racist by definition if not by intent, they become very sensitive. They forget that they cannot be immune from the history of imperialism, colonialism, slavery, etc. That needs to be acknowledged, otherwise they will never realise the amount of racism that has been passed on to them by accident of history. (Student 40 HEI B).

Student	044	The racism in this institution is very subtle. Sometimes the racism I am talking about is not even apparent to some BME students. It is certainly not always apparent to White students or lecturers. At times when you mention that you have experienced racism, White friends and lecturers turn round and look surprised as if to say, how could you say such a thing, when we have been with you most of the time and we have not seen you experiencing racism. That's how subtle that racism is. As a result to be honest some BME students don't bother to raise issues of racism because it appears that you are just nit-picking and being petty. (Student 44 HEI B)
Student	055	What I found at times very upsetting and frustrating was that whenever there was a heavy discussion about the experiences of BME students or BME people in general with White female lecturers, invariably that subject would be quickly switched to a related or distant issue on gender or sexism. I am a positive BME woman. I know that sexism pervades most of these HEIs. Issues of gender and sexism are very closely linked, but I strongly object to the way that debates or discussions on racism tend to be high-jacked and thus marginalised, and yet issues of racism are very important to all BME students. (Student 55 HEI B)

HEI C

Student results	Code	
Student	070	At the University there is very little time when tutors have one-to-one relationship with students. In some cases the personal tutorial system has been completely cut off. This has created difficulties for BME students who would have benefited from the support and guidance that the personal tutorial system used to offer. This also would be a time when BME students would voice their problems and share their experiences, and at times would change the tutor's attitude and behaviour in the way they viewed and treated BME students. That opportunity has been lost. (Student 70 HEI C)
Student	078	HEIs from my experience are a facade of neutrality in dealing with the racial inequalities. Firstly, there are far too few BME academics on the teaching staff. White teachers learn about racism from text books, they don't live it, they hear and read about it. This is very frustrating as it leaves (once again) little room for the experiences of BME students to be brought into the debate. (Student 78 HEI C)

1 **Table 2.** HESA/OFFA Access Indicators - Widening Participation at
2 National Level

HESA (2012) and OFFA (2012) Access Indicators – Widening Participation (Direct Discrimination at National Level)	% Low Participation Neighbourhood – Direct Discrimination	% Lower Socio-Economic Groups – Direct Discrimination
Russell Group HEIs	4.3%	19.3%
Post 1990s HEIs	8.4%	23.2%
FE Colleges	11.3%	25%

3 **Figure 12.** Low Participation Rate for students from Widening
4 Participation Backgrounds - Direct Discrimination

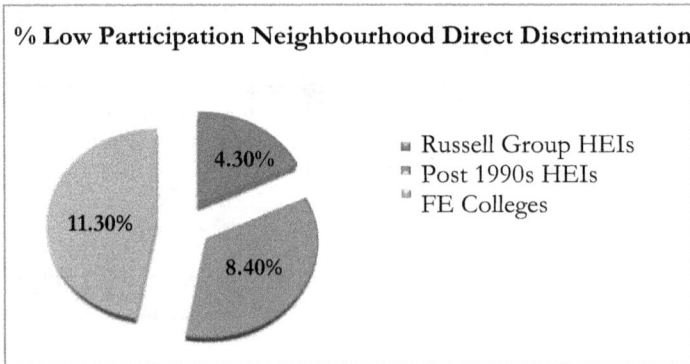

5

6 **Figure 13.** Student Participation Rate From Low Socio-Economic
7 Groups

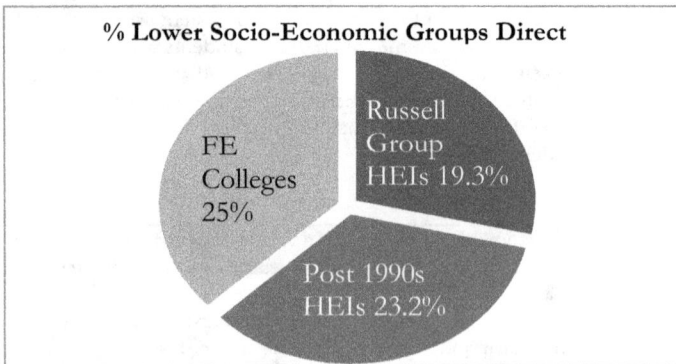

8

1   **Direct Discrimination**

2   Direct discrimination where individuals are identified negatively
3   because of their racial group are significant in HEIs A and C. However,
4   research carried out at Institutional Level within HEIs A and C
5   illustrate that widening participation although depicted as part of the
6   HEI policy does not reflect the statistics provided by HESA and OFFA
7   outlined in Table 3. Minority ethnic applicants are not shortlisted for
8   courses on the basis of their race, colour, nationality, ethnic origins,
9   with no scope for justification. The findings from HEI A, B and C
10   further suggest that indirect discrimination occurs within the HEI. The
11   Race Relations Amendment Act (2000) contains definitions of indirect
12   and direct discrimination. The Race Relations Amendment Act (2000)
13   stipulates that indirect racism should not exist in any form, particularly
14   where a person from a particular group is disadvantaged. Findings from
15   all three case study HEIs illustrate that the guidelines set out by the
16   Race Relations Amendment Act (2000) were not adhered to. Findings
17   from HEI A, B and C suggest that "institutionalised racism" exists to a
18   greater or lesser extent in all three case study HEIs. The Equality and
19   Diversity Act (2010) outlined in section states that discrimination in
20   any form should not exist.

21   **Figure 7.** Participation in the UK Higher Education HEIs -
22   Undergraduate Students By Ethnicity

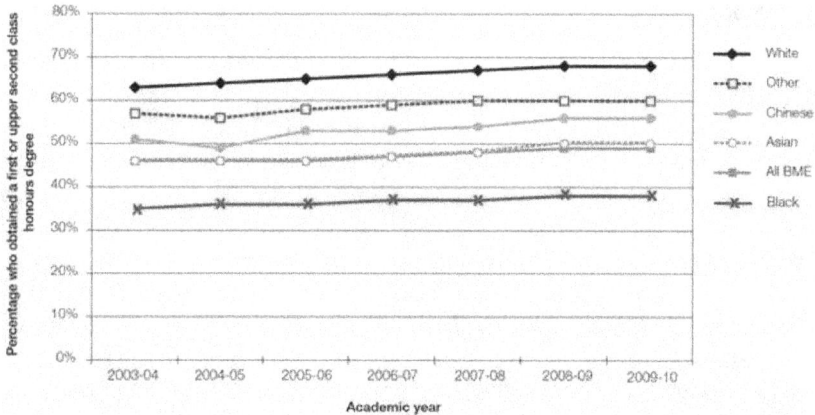

24   The findings from HEI A, B and C show a significant decline in
25   BME student participation within all three case study HEIs which does
26   not reflect the statistics outlined by HEFCE in Figure 14. Indirect
27   discrimination is significantly evident from findings where research
28   carried out within three case study HEIs showed that the number of

BME students obtaining a honours degree from each of the case study HEIs shows significantly reduced participation from students coming from BME backgrounds.

Table 3. Comparison of BME/White First and Upper Second Class Honours Degrees

Institution	BME	White
HEI A	33.9	66.1
HEI B	45.4	54.6
HEI C	25.4	74.6

Low representation of BME is identified within the three case study HEIs is against the Race Relations Amendment Act (2000) as outlined in Chapter two. Table 3 illustrates the low numbers of visible BME students. There is fundamentally under-representation of defined racial groups. Section 2.4 outlines that racism is a disregard of an individual's respect and dignity. The Race Relations Amendment Act (2000) stipulates again that individuals should be considered equal regardless of their colour, race and gender. Findings illustrated that BME students are considered failures regardless of their ability, and the basis of this is associated with race and colour.

Social Inclusion

The HEI sector in the 21st century is confronted with current and further complex challenges across the sphere. The concern surrounding global competitiveness within HEIs is now central to the functioning of neoliberal economic markets. Globalisation has meant that cross border initiatives have created greater social inclusion barriers. In the UK there has been a shift in HEI UK educational policy. There should be an increase in participation rates from those individuals who come from socially excluded backgrounds and that education should be open to all individuals with the right qualifications regardless of ethnicity. Regardless of the government's attempts to address social inclusion there are still significantly under-represented and disadvantaged groups within the level of participation. The coalition government is attempting to promote social inclusion by stating that students are at the heart of the system. Research analysis at the three case study HEIs highlighted data on students' choices, complying that while privately educated students identified primarily with elite HEIs such as Oxford and Cambridge, middle class state-

1 educated students had a strong preference for redbrick HEIs founded
2 prior to 1992, and those from working-class backgrounds felt most at
3 home in the newer HEIs, for example, former post-1992 HEIs, many
4 of which were granted university status in 1992.

5 **Table 4.** Social inclusion

Social inclusion		
HEI A		
Student results	**Code**	**Comments**
Student	008	There is no cultural belonging in this place. My example is me...why doesn't it show on my records that I used to be homeless and had no support from anywhere. My tutors should be monitoring me and asking me for meetings to make sure I feel OK about everything. My only support really is from friends of mine. That nurturing environment doesn't exist at this university and that nobody was interested in me in my first few weeks here really is an important statement. (Student 8 HEI A)
Student	012	The other students went into the labs and looked at the equipment and instantly knew what to do...I felt a bit isolated as I had never seen half of the stuff there. I think a lot of the students in the room had been to private school....I guess. I felt a little awkward and didn't want to touch anything just in case I looked stupid. (Student 12 HEI A)
Student	021	My White peers like to go on bar crawls when we have guest lectures or tutorials we tend to have a selection of alcoholic drinks, as I don't drink alcohol I feel it is harder to mix and feel accepted. So I tend to stand out from my peers and automatically feel isolated. (Student 21 HEI A)
HEI B		
Student results	**Code**	
Student	032	The university website shows a black student with a White girl and other colours and you think wow – but when you actually start studying it becomes pretty clear that there is no mix like that. You are given the impression that students mix and get on with each other from different backgrounds but in reality they don't. (Student 32 HEI B)
HEI C		
Student results	**Code**	
Student	066	We have limitations and are responsible for our household as we as having to study. Whereas the White students can go clubbing and partying and don't come across as having other family commitments....I have to take other things into

		consideration and basically I am judged by the community that I live in. It is hard. This is who I am and I have to show my family that I am a good son. My family have expectations which I have to meet and I can't push these expectations to one side. (student 66 HEI C)
Student	077	I was thrown out of my tutorial.... I thought I could go to the toilet walk in and out of the tutorial room if I wanted to.... I didn't think I needed to get permission. I went to answer a call and this tutor picked up my bag and put it outside of the room.... I was pretty upset about that.... I did make a complaint but nothing was ever done about it. I didn't get an apology or anything like that. (Student 77 HEI C)

Recruitment and retention

The government want to ensure that students from BME backgrounds attend and remain in HEI education to obtain their degree qualifications. The government has therefore put into place measures such as the Race Relations Amendment Act (2000), Higher Education White Paper (2011) Higher Education Act (2004), Equality and Diversity Act (2010), and the Learning and Skills Act (2000). However, regardless of the measures outlined above being put into place it was evident from research results in particular interview feedback that these measures were somewhat superficial.

Table 5. Changes to Student Number Controls

Changes to Student Number Controls Arising from the White Paper 2011	
Students with entry qualifications equivalent to AAB at A-level and above	All HEIs are free to recruit as many of the widening participation applicants as they wish in 2012-2013
	Removed from student number controls based on historic numbers in 2010-11 and an assumption of growth by 2012-13
	Estimation that the widening participation group would account for just over 85,000 of all entrants in 2012-13

Table 5 shows that widening participation students are required to have AAB at A level and above, this creates limitations as students from widening participation backgrounds who have not studied or obtained the grades outlined in table 6. Findings from the three case study HEIs illustrated that widening participation students and BME students coming from widening participation backgrounds had not obtained the qualifications outlined in table 5, which actually placed these students under considerable disadvantage. Findings from the three case study

1   HEIs are outlined in table 6.

2   **Table 6.** Case Study HEIs Findings for Widening Participation
3   Numbers in relation to Entry Qualifications

Case Study HEIs BME Widening Participation Numbers in relation to entry qualifications	
HEI A	10.8%
HEI B	16.5%
HEI C	13.5%

4   The findings outlined in table 6 signify that the government
5   widening participation agenda for social inclusion is not meetings
6   targets set out at national level and discussed in previous sections. A
7   considerable gap remains between those from BME backgrounds and
8   those from White middle class backgrounds.

9   **Learning Teaching and Assessment**

10   At the national level, the aim of government policy in the UK is to
11   put teaching, training, and learning at the forefront of the learning and
12   skills system. Using evidence from policy sources despite policy
13   rhetoric about the devolution of responsibility to the 'front line', the
14   dominant 'images' that government has of putting teaching, learning
15   and assessment at the heart of the Learning and Skills Sector involve a
16   narrow concept of learning and skills; an idealisation of learner agency
17   lacking an appreciation of the pivotal role of the learner/tutor
18   relationship and a top-down view of change in which central
19   government agencies are relied on to secure education standards.
20   Learning is conceived of in government texts as an individual activity,
21   whereas education is a collective activity that is the responsibility of
22   national government. This interpretation is supported by statements
23   contained in government documents, for example, 'putting learners at
24   the heart of the system' implies a clear focus on the recipients of the
25   service. The percentage of UK-domicile BME students studying in
26   higher education, at all levels, is statistically higher than that of White
27   students, with the proportion of UK-domicile BME students having
28   increased from 14.9% in 2003-04 to 18.1% in 2009-10 (HEFCE, 2011).
29   However, there are substantial differences in patterns of participation:
30   in general, more BME females participate in HE than males; Black
31   Caribbean and Bangladeshi participation rates are half those of Black
32   African and Indian participation rates, and Black students are both
33   older than other BME students and their White entrants. In addition
34   to the variable participation rates of BME students, the retention rates
35   of BME students are also uneven, with 91.1% of Chinese entrants likely

1 to continue or qualify compared to 90.4% of White students and only
2 88.7% of Black entrants. Of those who do remain in HE, there is a
3 significant gap in degree attainment between BME and White students
4 as measured by the percentage being awarded a first or upper second-
5 class degree.

6 Recent data evidence that 66.5% of White students studying first
7 degrees received a first or upper second class Honours degree, with
8 only 49.2% of BME students achieving this and 38.1% of Black
9 students, with research conducted by the DfES, showing that even
10 after controlling for the majority of contributory factors (prior
11 attainment, subject of study, age, gender, disability, deprivation, type of
12 HE institution attended, type of Level 3 qualifications, mode of study,
13 term-time accommodation and ethnicity), being from a minority ethnic
14 group (except the Other Black, Mixed and Other groups) was still
15 found to have a statistically significant and negative effect on degree
16 attainment. Research by the Higher Education Funding Council for
17 England (HEFCE) found that differences in the attainment between
18 White and BME groups could only in some small part be explained by
19 the differing profiles of the students.

20 **Table 7.** Learning Teaching and Assessment

Learning Teaching and Assessment		
HEI A		
Student results	**Code**	**Comments**
Student	003	We don't get the same marks as the White students. I've never seen a BME student get a first - I really can't tell you why but I always get a border mark of 67 to 68. I'm not saying that this is because our names are different and then we don't get the marks but maybe I'm not clever enough or maybe we misunderstand what the lecturer tells us? Maybe their work is better than ours. I don't know but sometimes I think they get different feedback than we do. They e-mail their tutors and get more out of them than we do – so maybe we should be a bit more proactive. (Student 3 HEI A) I have a good network of friends, and we tend to support each other. We try and motivate, guide and support each other, because we want to try and get a good grade and we don't really get anything back from the staff or our White peers. (Student 3 HEI A)

Student	008	When you start to look at people in terms of their skin colour and profile people then start to think about role models and how they fit into certain categories. There are then the perceptions that BME people are doing quite badly. Why is it that we have to be associated with black role models nobody ever mentions White role models... sometimes I think things are made more complicated than they need to be. (Student 8 HEI A)
Student	011	University lecturers are given time and this university and in fact bugger it – a lot of HEIs have not been proactive with us black students. I have friends at other HEIs who say the same they don't get the support and guidance in their assessments either like me I mean.... I ask so many questions but the tutor looks at me as if I am thick or something...from experience if you approach a lecturer they always say to me go and fill out an extension form or go and ask the counselling people. All I ask for his to be seen as an individual and not a black man in a White environment...cos this is sometimes I feel.....(Student 11 HEI A)
Student	024	I want to get a better job and this means so much to me for my children. I find that when I apply for anything I never get past the phone interview I feel so stupid. I challenged one company and they said that they had lots of people applying and that's why I didn't get it. (Student 24 HEI A)

HEI B

Student	**Code**
results	

Student	049	I would say that we don't seem to achieve the same grade levels as the White students. I've never seen a black or Asian student on my course getting a 2:1s... I always get a 67 or 68 mark and my feedback is never clear as to why I got the mark I did....um maybe I think... we are not that clever, I sometimes think that the White students work is better than ours maybe? Some of my White friends email their tutors more than I do maybe I should be more active. (Student 49 HEI B)

HEI C

Student	**Code**
results	

Student	068	You get a quick response when you email tutors on my course. My lecturers are pretty quick to respond to problems or questions I have. I really like my tutors they care about me or at least they show that they care about me. (Student 68 HEI C)

1   Student comments illustrated the level of difference they felt in all
2 aspects of their teaching, learning and assessments within the three case

1   study HEIs.

2   This chapter has aimed to critically discuss from the findings which
3   signify the gap in attainment throughout UK HEIs in terms of BME
4   engagement. The reasons behind the attainment gap are complex and
5   multi-faceted, structural, organisational, attitudinal, cultural and
6   financial. Findings in chapter four signify student and staff experiences.
7   Significantly marking practices, assessment, feedback, student lecturer
8   and peer interactions and how course design and pedagogic activities
9   might maximise student attainment. Concerns over segregation, low
10   teacher expectations, undervaluing and under challenging BME
11   students, prejudiced attitudes associated with linguistic competences
12   and discriminatory practice inherent in learning, teaching and
13   assessment activities and student support. The discussion from each of
14   the five themes generated in chapter four, have been within this chapter
15   analytically discussed extensively. As a result of the findings in chapter
16   four and analytical discussion in chapter five, chapter six will present
17   the Social Inclusion Framework Model (SIF).

CHAPTER 10

CONCLUSIONS AND RECOMMENDATIONS

This chapter sets out the conclusions to the notion of CRT within HEIs. There are five key areas where the book endeavours to outline and highlight the impact of CRT within HEIs for BME students (Ladson-Billings, 2009). These are:

- Critical Race Theory presence in HEIs

- Race and Racism

- Social Inclusion

- Learning Teaching and Assessment

Recruitment and Retention Firstly, CRT was examined and how it has a fundamental presence in HEIs. An important aspect that was raised in terms of CRT was that race, gender and class are socially constructed and, more importantly, they determine the haves and the have-nots in society (Allen, 2017). They also provide the main principles of social organisations and institutions in society; and they produce and maintain social hierarchy among different racial and ethnic, gender, and class groups. Secondly, the impact of race and racism were examined in terms of BME social inclusion, BME learning, teaching and assessment and the recruitment and retention of BME students within HEIs (Bimper, 2017).

The following conclusions and recommendations have been made: The SIF model identifies that at national, institutional and operational levels there is a requirement for a robust set of interactions addressing BME concerns (Giraldo, Huerta, & Solorzano, 2017). At national level; HEFCE and OFFA need to work closely with HEIs to create social inclusion in terms of BME requirements, taking into consideration working with HEIs to develop a clear and concise widening participation policy, which encompasses:

- A clear and concise widening participation policy for all HEIs

- A true reflection of funding in terms of allowing HEIs to fulfil the social inclusion requirements

Figure 14. Social Inclusion Framework Model (SIF)

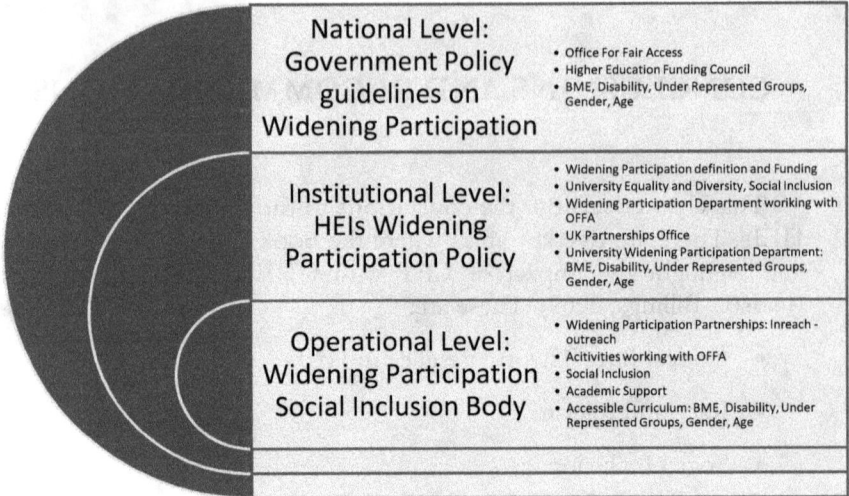

National Level: Government Policy guidelines on Widening Participation	• Office For Fair Access • Higher Education Funding Council • BME, Disability, Under Represented Groups, Gender, Age
Institutional Level: HEIs Widening Participation Policy	• Widening Participation definition and Funding • University Equality and Diversity, Social Inclusion • Widening Participation Department working with OFFA • UK Partnerships Office • University Widening Participation Department: BME, Disability, Under Represented Groups, Gender, Age
Operational Level: Widening Participation Social Inclusion Body	• Widening Participation Partnerships: Inreach - outreach • Acitivies working with OFFA • Social Inclusion • Academic Support • Accessible Curriculum: BME, Disability, Under Represented Groups, Gender, Age

- Work closely with the university equality and diversity teams within the HEIs to ensure that social inclusion is being addressed practically as well as theoretically

- HEI widening participation departments should be required to work closely with OFFA to ensure they are meeting national level objectives

- Each HEI is required to work with an established Partnerships office

- National and institutional level widening participation departments working with admissions.

- At operational level as the SIF model outlines each HEI school should have a transparent understanding of the term widening participation as well as the necessity to address social inclusion

Operational level to be successful with preceding widening participation needs:

- Academic support in terms of recruitment and retention

- A socially inclusive curriculum

- Administrative and academic training

- BME staff recruitment in order to create role models for BME students

The SIF model aims to increase diversity and enhancing BME attainment which should also be utilised to help drive change. Within such a competitive market, students will increasingly make choices based on the quality of provision, value for money and graduate outcomes (Gilborn, Warmington, & Denmack, 2018). Those HEIs who maximise the attainment of all students, including BME students, are likely to attract more consumers of higher education.

As the SIF model dictates the commitment for social inclusion and widening participation policy change should be led from the top and be written into UK HEIs strategic plans (Blaisdell, 2019). The SIF model outlines that in order to minimise the attainment gap there is a requirement to develop a partnership approach between staff and BME students, involving local Students Unions and the National Union of Students; BME students should be regarded as co-producers of knowledge and success; consultation with BME students' needs to be systematic; structures have to be put in place to ensure communication and practice takes place (Daftary, 2018). All staff, pastoral, administrative and academic need to be equipped with the skills and confidence to build relationships with BME students; in particular, clear and specific guidance and training for personal tutors should be put into place. Staff should make sure that BME students understand exactly what is expected of them – in relation to academic attitudes, participation and the production of work; however, BME students should be empowered to challenge poor practice and clarify feedback (Christian, Seamster, & Ray, 2019).

Fair marking practices should be implemented as depicted in the SIF model clear and transparent assessment guidelines; offering a choice of assessments; providing exemplars of first-class assignments; aligning module marks against dissertation marks; anonymous marking; scrutinising both assignments and marking for cultural biases. In addition, assignment briefs should always be undertaken in the context of a discussion-based activity (James & Russell, 2019).

Peer-assisted learning and peer mentoring could include a focus on understanding degree classifications, including what might be required to be successful at each level of degree, understanding assessment requirements and interpreting feedback, and how to challenge lecturers (Gillborn, 2020). BME students should be provided with examples of good coursework at different levels, given opportunities to mark themselves and each other and be involved in designing induction programmes (Matsuda, 2018). A holistic, longitudinal approach should be taken to reduce the attainment gap, from pre-entry aspiration raising activities through to progression to post-graduation study and/or employment. Where targeted interventions are deemed to be desirable, a clear rationale for such activity should be communicated to both staff and students. Initiatives designed to reduce the attainment gap should, in principle, be based on clear evidence and have timely and measurable outcomes (Ladson-Billings, 2009). All students should be viewed as partners in the educational journey and systematically involved in the design and implementation of inclusive learning, teaching and assessment activities. Institutions should put strategies in place to ensure that staff are able, and empowered, to develop effective relationships with all BME students; these relationships should be built on a sharing of power and responsibility (Flores, 2017).

Academic development and support should be largely mainstreamed and BME students should be encouraged and empowered to draw on these existing mechanisms; however, institutions also need to implement alternative strategies to support those students unable or unwilling to access mainstream provision. Institutional strategies should be implemented to enable staff to develop sufficient confidence to deal with issues of race and racism; both staff and students should be afforded safe spaces within which to discuss race and racism (Goessling, 2018). All teaching staff should set local targets for reducing the gap; good practice in teaching and learning, leading to enhanced student success, should be recognised and valued institutionally. BME students are distributed in a disparate manner across HEIs (Annamma, Ferri, & Connor, 2018).

The focus of CRT has been the fundamental themes throughout this study in terms race and racism, recruitment and retention, social inclusion, learning, teaching and assessment strategies and in the fundamental development of the SIF model. CRT can be used as a means of addressing BME student concerns within HEIs (Allen, 2017). HEIs should strive to create inclusive learning models through formulating diversity initiatives, develop a robust infrastructure of social inclusion. It is fundamental to use CRT concepts to help develop racial equality within UK HEIs (Lavender, 2019). A significant factor for the use of critical race theory tenets is that it is intertwined with the four key themes within the research study (Adams, 2017). It is essential for academics, administrators and BME students to work collaboratively for social inclusion to work.

The evidence from findings suggests that, despite the rhetoric of standards for all, education policy in the UK is actively involved in the defence, legitimation and extension of institutional racism (Flores, 2017). The assumptions which feed, and are strengthened by, this view, are not overtly discriminatory but their effects are empirically verifiable and materially real in every meaningful sense. Shaped by long-established cultural, economic and historical structures of racial domination, the continued promotion of policies and practices that are known to be racially divisive testifies to tacit intentionality in the system (Moodley, Mujtaba, & Kleiman, 2017). The racist outcomes of contemporary policy may not be coldly calculated but they are far from accidental.

A CRT perspective allows for the recognition that racism is a normal and common aspect that shapes society. Race is deeply embedded in social, cultural and political structures, therefore making it difficult to recognise and address (Allen, 2017). Race is socially constructed with historical interpretations that marginalise BME students. Therefore, colour blind racism and racial indifferences must consistently be challenged through exposing the manner in which racial advances often come at the cost of promoting or feeding into White self-interests (Ladson-Billings, 2009). Moreover, colour blind ideologies ignore the systemic nature of race, excuse accountability for racial injustices and promote apathetic, covert acts of racism, which ultimately place power and privilege with the dominant group. In 2009 Ladson-Billings argued that CRT could be helpful in unmasking and exposing racism in its various permutations within education. From findings and discussions it is imperative that this strategy should be applied to student development theories. The introduction of CRT as a framework in which issues of race and social educational inequalities were at the foreground in HEIs. It is significant to note here that CRT is interdisciplinary in its approach because it incorporates various intellectual traditions that promote racial justice. Further to this, findings suggest that CRT should be employed in higher education and student affairs to illuminate racial inequalities and hierarchies and be implemented to transform HEIs (Allen, 2017). Additionally, findings signify a conceptualised analogy which is important to address within the case study HEIs as depicted below:

- Race continues to be a significant factor in determining inequality within higher education

- UK society is based on property rights

- The intersection of race and property creates an analytical tool through which inequalities can be understood

Race continues to be a significant factor in producing inequalities in society and educational institutions. Moreover, BME students are more likely to lag behind that of their White counter-parts (Huber, Gonzalez, & Solorzano, 2018). BME students are more likely to drop out from their studies. They are more inclined to follow vocational programmes of study and leave universities with lower classifications. BME students are more likely to have difficulties enrolling within HEIs because of previous deficiencies created by an educational system where inequalities between the rich and the poor persist (Hurtardo, 2019). It is imperative for educators and administrative staff to understand how race produces inequalities. Racism is at the core of the curriculum which focuses exclusively on White, Western viewpoints that render BME students invisible in what is learned and discussed (Jackson & Barton, 2017). BME students are significantly underrepresented because they often experience isolation and marginalisation. Race is especially evident when BME students experience cultural assaults such as discrimination and stereotyping. These assaults are seen as racial micro-aggressions or subtle insults which are verbal and non-verbal.

It is important to signify here that race is a reality when BME students do not feel safe, welcome or comfortable in an institutional environment which marginalises them (Jackson & Barton, 2017). Therefore, HEIs should incorporate an inclusive curriculum that incorporates a dialogue of race. Ethnic culture centres could be offered as places where BME students from specific racial groups can meet, share resistance and form communities (Gilborn, Warmington, & Denmack, 2018). These centres can be considered as counter-spaces where students can retreat from harsh campus racial climates and micro-aggressions that is subtle, verbal and nonverbal or insults. HEIs are based around the concept of having property rights. HEI academics and administrators and structures use a critical race lens and need to address the issue fundamentally (Garcia & Velez, 2018). Academics own the curriculum and design it according to their own ontological and epistemological assumptions, which, as findings for this study dictate are against BME students (Adams, 2017).

Faculties subscribe to mono-cultural colour-blind paradigms that validate western structures of knowledge, individual achievement, rationality, exclusivity, and the subjugation of knowledge created by BME individuals (Hallmon, Anaza, Sandoval, & Fernandez, 2020).

1 There are racial inequalities that cannot be ignored with regard to
2 institutional leadership. For example, the leadership team within HEIs
3 have the right to make final decisions and move the institution in a
4 particular way. There is a need for a connection to exist between both
5 distribution of power and influence more equitably. The most harmful
6 notion which was evident from findings was the concept that
7 Whiteness was the ultimate property (Hallmon, Anaza, Sandoval, &
8 Fernandez, 2020). The view being that what Whites own academically
9 is what constitutes success. Therefore, if BME students conform to
10 White viewpoints, they are rewarded and those BME students who
11 choose not to follow this analogy are considered as perpetrators
12 (Hawkins, Carter-Francique, & Cooper, 2016). BME students
13 conformed to White norms, such as speech patterns, dress and
14 behaviours they would be viewed through a different lens than those
15 who chose to continue to follow their own constructs within society
16 (Garcia & Velez, 2018). CRT perspective should understand that within
17 the HEI setting, Whites are given advantages in a number of ways. For
18 example, BME students felt that being White carried more status and
19 power than being a BME.

20 The classroom environment - BME students sit together in class
21 they are viewed as segregating themselves, while Whites who exhibit
22 this behaviour are considered to be socialising with friends (Bimper,
23 2017). Moreover, BME students who dress in clothes representing their
24 culture and speak a language other than English experience cultural
25 assaults in the form of discrimination and stereotypes (Goessling,
26 2018). It is therefore essential that educators and administrators
27 become more cognizant of the numerous ways in which the
28 experiences, languages and cultures of BME students are minimised
29 within the case study HEI settings and seek to transform perceptions,
30 practices and policies that privilege some students at the expense of
31 others (Graham, et al., 2019).

32 To conclude, it is imperative that as educators and administrators
33 we challenge, question and critique traditional theoretical perspectives
34 (Hallmon, Anaza, Sandoval, & Fernandez, 2020). Many of the theories
35 that are used to guide practice do not pay any real attention to race.
36 Therefore, there is a need

37 that we continuously engage in critical examinations that provide
38 an accurate context of the theorist's backgrounds, identities and
39 assumptions, how socio-political and historical contexts,
40 privilege and power may have shaped the theory, and the

applicability of the theory to various student populations (Gillborn, 2020).

There is a need for staff to be open to moving beyond the status quo and recognising the entrenchment of race in educational settings, including programs and services offered. Findings signified that all too often staff had a tendency to perpetuate the status quo, or one group's construction of what is normal without having looked more deeply at the role of race (Bimper, 2017). Consistently ignoring race and its systemic complexities further disadvantages BME students. When the complexity of professional actions is recognised only then can there be a movement towards social justice (Gillborn, 2020). It is fundamental that faculties and staff throughout HEI environments recognise and become more knowledgeable and aware of the importance of the classroom and HEI campus environment. In essence, academics must be cognizant of the factors that guide decisions on the curriculum, particularly what will and will not be taught and how the material is presented (Howard & Navarro, 2016). Academics should reflect on how racial perspectives are incorporated into reading materials, class discussions and assignments. Academics should be mindful of the roles that race, power and privilege play in classroom dynamics.

Actively incorporating a critical race perspective in daily practice is essential. With this in consideration, academics and administrative staff approach their work with an awareness of the existence of race and the different ways that people experience realities (Annamma, Ferri, & Connor, 2018). They are thus clearer about the ways in which race continues to produce societal inequalities. Finally, by following this analogy academics and administrative staff can understand how the intersection of race with other social identities presents a clearer picture that is necessary for working with BME students (Giraldo, Huerta, & Solorzano, 2017) (Branchu & Robbins, 2019). Both academics and administrative staff need to be knowledgeable about and aware of their own racial identities, honestly evaluate themselves in terms of their understanding of race and racism and recognise how their knowledge, awareness and racial identity influence their decisions, policies and interactions with students from diverse backgrounds.

References

Adams, B. (2017). Black Lives/ White Backgrounds: Claudia Rankine's Citizen: An American Lyric and Critical Race Theor. *Comparative American Studies An International Journal, 15*(1-2), 54-71.

Allen, M. (2017). The relevance of critical race theory: Impact on students of colour. *Urban Education Research and Policy Annuals, 5*(1).

Anderson, T., & Shattuck, J. (2013). Design-Based Research: A decade of progress in education research? . *Educational research*, 16-25.

Annamma, S., Ferri, B. A., & Connor, D. J. (2018). Cultivating and expanding disability critical race theory (DisCrit). *Manifestos for the Future of Critical Disability Studies 1.*

Anyon, Y., Lechuga, C., Downing, B., Greer, E., & Simmons, J. (2018). An exploration of the relationships between student racial background and the school sub-contexts of office discipline referrals: A critical race theory analysis. *Race Ethnicity and Education, 21*(3), 390-406.

Barnes, M. L. (2016). Empirical methods and critical race theory: A discourse on possibilities for a hybrid methodology. *Wis. L. Rev*, 443.

Bimper, J. R. (2017). Mentorship ob black student-athletes at a predominately white American University: Critical race theory perspective on student athlete development. *Education and Society, 22*(2), 175-193.

Blaisdell, B. (2019). Seeing with Poetic eyes: Critical race theory and moving from liberal to critical forms of race research in sociology of education.

Blessing, L. T., & Chakrabarti, A. (2009). A design Research Methodology .

Borrell, L. N. (2018). Critical Race Theory: Why Should We Care about Applying It in our Research? *Ethnicity and Disease*, 215.

Bradbury, A. (2020). A critical race theory framework for educational policy analysis: the case of bilingual learners and assessment policy in England. *Race Ethnicity and Education, 23*(2), 241-260.

Branchu, C., & Robbins, D. (2019). "A Commentary on Althusser's 1963 Presentation of Bourdieu and Passeron" Theory, Culture & Society. (Vol. 36).

Brown, A. L., Brown, K. D., & Ward, A. (2017). Critical race theory meets culturally relevant pedagogy: Advancing a critical sociohistorical consciousness for teaching and curriculum. *Social Education, 81*(1), 23-27.

Bush, A. A., McLaughlin, J. E., & White, C. (2018). Response to Critical Race Theory for Pharmacy Diversity Curriculum. *American Journal of pharmaceutical education,, 82*(2).

Cabrera, N. L. (2018). Where is the Racial Theory in Critical Race Theory? A constructive criticism of Curtis. *The Review of Higher Education*, 209-233.

Carrera, N. L. (2019). Critical Race Theory v Deficit Models. *Equity and Excellence in Education, 52*(1), 47-54.

Case, J. M., & Light, G. (2011). Emerging Research Methodologies in engineering education research. *Journal of Engineering Education*, 186-210.

Case, J. M., & Light, G. (2011). Emerging research methodologies in engineering education research. *Journal of Engineering Education*, 186-210.

Caspers, I. B. (2019). Afrofuturism, critical race theory, and policing in the Year 2044. *NYUL Revv*, 1.

Chang, E. (2020). Book Review: Born out of struggle: Critical race theory, school creation, and the politics of interruption.

Chapman, T. K., & DeCuir-Gunby, J. T. (2018). A Future Agenda for Understanding Critical Race Research Methods and Methodologies. *Understanding Critical Race Research Methods and Methodologies: Lessons from the Field.*

Chapman, T. K., Contreras, F., Martinez, J. E., & Rodgigiez, G. M. (2020). High Achieving African American Students and the College Choice Process: Applying Critical Race Theory.

Christian, M., Seamster, L., & Ray, V. (2019). New directions in critical race theory and sociology: Racism, white supremacy and resistance. *American behavioural scientist., 23*(2), 1731-1740.

Daftary, A. H. (2018). Critical race theory: An effective framework for social work research, *Journal of Ethnic and Cultural Diversity in Social Work*, 1-16.

Davis, J., & Jett, C. C. (2019). Critical Race Theory in Mathematics Education.

Delgado, R., & Stefancic, J. (2017). *Critical race theory: An Introduction* (Vol. 20). NYU Press.

Dixon, A. D., James, A., & Frieson, B. L. (2018). Critical Race Theory, Participatory Research and Social Justice. *Understanding Critical Race Research Methods and Methodologies: Lessons from the Field.*

Dixson, A. D., & Rousseau, A. (2018). Where are we? Critical race theory in education 20 years later. *Peabody Journal of Education, 93*(1), 121-131.

Flintoff, A. (2014). Tales from the playing field: Black Minority Ethnic Students' experiences of physical education teacher education. *Race Ethnicity and Education*, 346-366.

Flores, L. A. (2017). Critical race theory. The International Encyclopedia of Intercultural Communication. 1-5.

Garcia, N. M., & Velez, V. N. (2018). QuantCrit: Rectifying quantitative methods through critical race theory.

Gilborn, D., Warmington, P., & Denmack, S. (2018). QuantCrit: education, policy, 'Big Data' and principles for a critical race theory of statistics. *Race Ethnicity and Education, 2*(2), 158-179.

Gillborn, D. (2020). The White Bones of Policy: Structure, Agency and a Vulture's-Eye View of Critical Race Theory. *Knowledge, Policy and Practice in Education and the Struggle for Social Justice.*, 115.

Giraldo, L. G., Huerta, A. H., & Solorzano, D. (2017). From incarceration to community college: funds of knowledge, community cultural wealth, and critical race theory. *In Funds of Knowledge in Higher Education.*, 48-65.

Goessling, K. P. (2018). Increasing the depth of field: Critical race theory and photovoice as counter storytelling praxis. *The Urban Review, 50*(4), 648-674.

Graham, D. L., Alvarez, A. J., Heck, D. I., Rand, J. K., Milner, I. H., Anderson, A., ... Rogers, R. (2019). Critical Race Theory in Teacher Education: Informing Classroom Culture and Practice. *Teachers College Press.*

Hallmon, A., Anaza, E., Sandoval, A., & Fernandez, M. (2020). Black mothers, recreational choices for their children: a critical race theory story. *Annals of Leisure Research*, 1-15.

Hawkins, B. J., Carter-Francique, A. R., & Cooper, J. N. (2016). Critical Race Theory. *Palgrave Macmillan US.*

Henson, R. K., Hull, D. M., & Williams, C. S. (2010). Methodology in our education research culture: Toward a stronger collective quantitative proficiency. *Educational Researcher*, 229-240.

Howard, T. C., & Navarro, O. (2016). Critical race theory 20 years later: Where do we go from here? *Urban Education, 51*(3), 315-342.

Huber, L. P., Gonzalez, L. C., & Solorzano, D. G. (2018). Considerations for Using Critical Race Theory and Critical Content Analysis: A Research Note. *Understanding and Dismantling Privilege.*, 8-26.

Hurtardo, A. (2019). Critical Race Theory and Questioning Whiteness: Young

1   Feminists Speak Out Against Race and Class Privilege. *Frontiers: A Journal of*
2   *Women Studies, 40*(3), 90-116.
3   Jackson, C. C., & Barton, M. H. (2017). Power of Whiteness: Critical Race Theory
4   and Words in 'Get Out' and 'Detroit'. Southern Utah University.
5   James, A. M., & Russell, C. (2019). Tribal Critical Race Theory. Critical Race Theory
6   and in Teacher Education: Informing Classroom Culture and Practices,, 82.
7   Johnson-Ahorlu, R. N. (2017). Efficient social justice: How critical race theory
8   research can inform social movement strategy development. *The Urban Review,*
9   *49*(5), 729-745.
10   Kennedy, D. (2017). Intersectionality and Critical Race Theory: A Genealogical Note
11   from a CLS Point of View.
12   Ladson-Billings, G. (2009). *Critical Race Theory in Education.* Routledge.
13   Lavender, I. (2019). Critical race theory. *In Routledge Companion to Cyberpunk Culture,*
14   308-316.
15   Lee, A. J., Harrell, M., Villarreal, M., & White, D. (2020). The Value of Teaching
16   Critical Race Theory in Prison Spaces: Centering Students' Voices in Pedagogy.
17   *Humanities, 9*(2), 41.
18   Matsuda, M. J. (2018). Words that wound: Critical race theory, assaultive speech, and
19   the first amendment. Routledge.
20   Mattews, A. (2019). Racialized Youth and the Public Library: A Critical Race Theory
21   Approach to Program Utilization and Effectiveness.
22   Mensah, F. M. (2019). Finding voice and passion: Critical race theory methodology in
23   science teacher education. *American Educational Research Journal, 56*(4), 1412-1456.
24   Mills, K. A., & Unsworth, L. (2018). The Multimodal construction of race: a review
25   of critical race theory research. *Languages and Education*, 313-332.
26   Moodley, R., Mujtaba, F., & Kleiman, S. (2017). Critical race theory and mental
27   health. *Routledge International Handbook of Critical Mental Health*, 79-88.
28   Moschel, M. (2019). Critical race theory. In Research Handbook on Critical Legal
29   Theory. *Edward Elgar Publishing.*
30   Moustakas, C. (1990). Heuristic Research: Design, methodology, and applications.
31   Ogbonnaya-Ogburu, I. F., Smith, A. D., To, A., & Toyama, K. (2020). Critical Rache
32   Theory for HCI. *In Proceedings of the 2020 CHI Conference on Human Factors in*
33   *Computing Systems*, 1-16.
34   Parker, L. (2019). Race is....race isn't: Critical race theory and qualitative studies in
35   education. Routledge.
36   Patton, L. D. (2016). Disrupting postsecondary prose: Towards a critical race theory
37   of higher education. *Urban Education*, 315-342.
38   Perez Huber, L., & Solorzano, D. G. (2018). Teaching racial Microaggressions:
39   implications of critical race hypos for social work praxis. *Journal of Ethnic and*
40   *Cultural Diversity in Social Work, 27*(1), 54-71.
41   Polite, F. G., & Santiago, J. E. (2017). Social Responsibility/accountability addressing
42   constructs of critical race theory. *In Critical race theory: Black athletic sporting*
43   *experiences in the United States*, 279-293.
44   Ray, V. E., Randolph, A., Underhill, M., & Luke, D. (2017). Critical race theory,
45   Afro-pessimism, and racial progress narratives. *Sociology of Race and Ethnicity*, 147-
46   158.
47   Rector-Aranda, A. (n.d.). School Norms and Reforms, Critical Race Theory and the
48   Fairytale of Equitable Education. *Critical Questions in Education, 7*(1).
49   Reynolds, R., & Mayweather, D. (2017). Recounting racism, resistance, and
50   repression: Examining the experiences and #hashtag activism of college students
51   with critical race theory and counternarratives. *86*(3), 283-304.

1   Richards, D. A., Awokoya, J. T., Bridges, B. K., & Clark, C. (2018). One Size Does
2   Not Fit All: A Critical Race Theory Perspective on College Rankings. *The Review*
3   *of Higher Education, 42*(1), 269-312.
4   Rollock, N., & Dixson, A. D. (2016). Critical race theory. *The Wiley Blackwell*
5   *Encyclopedia of Gender and Sexuality Studies*, 1-6.
6   Rosiek, J. (2019). Critical race theory meets posthumanism: Lessons from a study of
7   racial resegregation in public schools. *Race Ethnicity and Education, 22*(1), 73-92.
8   Sablan, J. R. (2019). Can you really measure that? Combining critical race theory and
9   quantitative methods. *American educational research journal*, 178-203.
10 Saito, N. T., & Kinnison, A. J. (2020). Critical Race Theory and Children's Rights. . In
11   *The Oxford Handbook of Children's Rights Law.*
12 Sargent, J., & Casey, A. (n.d.). Appreciative inquiry for physical education and sport
13   pedagogy research: a methodological illustration through teachers' uses of digital
14   technology. *Sport, Education and Society*, 1-13.
15 Singer, J. N., & Garner, J. R. (2017). Fraternal Twins: Critical Race Theory and
16   Systematic Racism Theory as Analytic and Activist Tools for College Sport
17   Reform. *In Critical Race Theory: Black Athletic Sporting Experiences in the United States.*,
18   11-55.
19 Sleeter, C. E. (2017). Critical race theory and the whiteness of teacher education.
20   (Vol. 52). Urban Education.
21 Solarzano, D. G. (n.d.). A Freirean Journey from Chicana and Chicano Studies to
22   Critical Race Theory. *The Wiley Handbook of Paulo Freire*, 417-429.
23 Solorzano, D. G. (2019). Toward a Critical Race Theory for Teacher Education.
24   Teacher Preparation at the Intersection of Race and Poverty in Today's Schools.
25 Spinuzzi, C. (2005). The Methodology of Participatory Design. *Technical*
26   *Communication*, 163-174.
27 Spinuzzi, C. (2005). The methodology of participatory design. *Technical communication*,
28   163-174.
29 Stovall, D. (2018). Critical Race Theory, Jazz Methodology and the Struggle for
30   Justice in Education. *Understanding Critical Race Research Methods and Methodologies:*
31   *Lessons from the field.*
32 Stovall, D. O. (2016). Born out of struggle: Critical race theory, school creation, and
33   the politics of interruption.
34 Stovell, D. (2016). Out of adolesence and into adulthood: Critical Race theory,
35   retrenchment and the imperative of praxis. *Urban Education, 5*(3), 274-286.
36 Su, C. (2017). Beyond Inclusion: Critical race theory and participatory budgeting.
37   *39*(1), 126-142.
38 Trazo, T. A., & Kim, W. (2019). "Where Are You From?" Using Critical Race Theory
39   to Analyse Graphic Novel Counter-Stories of the Racial Microaggressions
40   Experienced by Two Angry Asian Girls. (Vol. 3). Intersections: Critical Issues in
41   Education.
42 Turner, T. L., Balmer, D. F., & Coverdale, J. H. (2013). Methodologies and study
43   designs relevant to medical education research. *International Review of Psychiatry*,
44   301-310.
45 Walls, L. (2016). Awakening a dialogue: A critical race theory analysis of US nature of
46   science research from 1967 to 2013. *Journal of Research in Science Teaching, 53*(10),
47   1546-1570.
48 Yao, C. W., George, M. C., & Malaney, B. V. (2019). Exploring the intersection of
49   transnationalism and critical race theory: a critical race analysis of international
50   student experiences in the United States. *Race Ethnicity and Education, 22*(1), 38-58.
51 Younger, K., Gascoine, L., Menzies, V., & Torgerson, C. (2019). A systematic review

of evidence on the effectiveness of interventions and strategies for widening participation in higher education. *Journal of Further and Higher Education*, 742-773.

Zhu, G., Peng, Z., & Qui, S. (2019). Extending critical race theory to Chinese education: Affordance and constraints. *A Journal of Comparative and International Education, 49*(5), 837-850.

1

www.ingramcontent.com/pod-product-compliance
Lightning Source LLC
Chambersburg PA
CBHW070348270326
41926CB00017B/4040

* 9 7 8 1 9 1 2 9 9 7 4 6 6 *